Walk Alone Together

Portrait of a French-English Marriage

A. Margaret Caza

to Louise
Many thanks,
Margaret

a. Margaret Cas

Stoddart

to Renaud

Copyright © 1990 by Margaret Caza

First published in 1990 by
Stoddart Publishing Co. Limited
34 Lesmill Road
Toronto, Canada
M3B 2T6

CANADIAN CATALOGUING IN PUBLICATION DATA

Caza, A. Margaret
    Walk alone together

ISBN 0-7737-2430-3 (bound) ISBN 0-7737-5371-0 (pbk.)

1. Caza, A. Margaret. 2. Wives - Québec (Province) -
Biography. 3. St. Anicet (Québec) - Biography.
4. Country life - Québec (Province) - St. Anicet -
Biography. I. Title.

FC2949.S2192Z49 1990   306.81'092   C90-093975-3
F1054.5.S2192C3 1990

Typesetting: Tony Gordon Ltd.

Printed in the United States of America

to Renaud

First published in 1990 by
Stoddart Publishing Co. Limited
34 Lesmill Road
Toronto, Canada
M3B 2T6

CANADIAN CATALOGUING IN PUBLICATION DATA

Caza, A. Margaret
    Walk alone together

ISBN 0-7737-2430-3 (bound) ISBN 0-7737-5371-0 (pbk.)

1. Caza, A. Margaret. 2. Wives - Québec (Province) - Biography. 3. St. Anicet (Québec) - Biography.
4. Country life - Québec (Province) - St. Anicet - Biography. I. Title.

FC2949.S2192Z49 1990   306.81'092   C90-093975-3
F1054.5.S2192C3 1990

Typesetting: Tony Gordon Ltd.

Printed in the United States of America

Walk Alone Togeth

Portrait of a French-English Marr

A. Margaret Caza

to Louise
Many thanks
Margaret

A. Margaret Cas

Stoddart

Contents

* * * * ○ * * * *

PART ONE

This House Will Be a Home

* * * * * ○ * * * *

CHAPTER 1

The Care and Feeding of a Compromise

It's a good thing Renaud and I married when we did, back before computer dating, plastic credit, equal rights and two-income families. I'd be too scared to marry today.

Though it took daring even then. In those days marriage meant spending thirty, forty, fifty years with the same person. Obviously I wasn't all that sure of our chances in the first place, or I wouldn't, with an almost-engagement-ring on my finger, have gone to work as a secretary at an airbase in Greenland during the summer of 1952.

After all, what did I know about this intense-eyed French-man, who had me hovering on the brink of turning my life inside out? I knew that he was Roman Catholic to my Protestant faith, French to my English and rural to my urban. I also knew that enough people with pursed lips and no sense of humor had sucked in their breaths and warned us we were headed for trouble.

Warn they did, but nobody suggested how to adjust, except for an airman in my office in Greenland, who was also preparing for marriage (preparing his fiancée is more like it) by telling her what was expected of her. She was taking Catholic instruction and sewing lessons (and probably learning how to be obedient, because it was plain that he expected no trouble from her).

I was greener than most brides-to-be and more confident than our situation warranted as I flew back from my job in the North, bolstered by a packet of Renaud's wonderful letters, and savoring the delicious suspension between past and future; between being single and being married.

As it turned out, being married was a lot like racing hand-in-hand downhill through a field of fragrant wildflowers and pulling up short at an unexpected obstacle course. At the summit of that hill, glowing crisply in the November air, was the great old stone church in St. Anicet, southwest of Montreal. Two weeks after I returned from Greenland Renaud and I stood in the presbytery next to this church (because Catholic teaching at the time wouldn't allow us to be married in the church), and Father Paul Deguire said, "I now pronounce you man and wife." Renaud eagerly agreed to love, honor and cherish me, even though the barbed wire, hurdles and water hazards of that obstacle course began when I borrowed his newly purchased second-hand grey Pontiac to drive there with my father, and we got side-swiped by a lumber truck twenty minutes before the ceremony and two miles short of the church.

This got us off to a late and red-faced start that set the pace, because being married didn't mean the two of us retiring to cosy little corners to work out neat compromises whenever we felt like beaning each other, which was often.

After the ceremony, there was a dry wedding reception at my parents' Montreal home, followed by a four-day New York City honeymoon and the happy job of settling into a small pre-fab rented bungalow in an old wartime explosives plant village with the apt name of Nitro.

Life was busy and fun. Monday to Friday we sprang out of bed and went off to work together. We visited and partied and let housework accumulate without remorse, until full sinks and laundry hampers forced us to clean up — often at 3:00 A.M. We lived as spontaneously as a pair of hiccups bouncing hand-in-hand through a wind tunnel, with reality loping toward us on a collision course.

Marriage to Renaud meant that I was married, if not to his religion, at least to his business ambitions, which I understood and appreciated — eventually; his political affiliations, which I waxed hot and cold over at the municipal, provincial and federal levels; the local watering hole, which I didn't even try to understand; a spirited social life; an entire small, totally French farm community, whose language baffled me; and the influence of a great-great ancestor by the name of Jean-Baptiste LeBeau-dit-Caza, who was among the first pioneer settlers to found the tightly knit community of St. Anicet. Generations of farm families in the village shared one heritage, an anchor holding them to a cherished past. It was a past that had nothing to do with me.

There was also brother-in-law Maurice, a jovial soul who started every sentence with "Sonofabitch . . ." and/or "Chris' . . ." and cousin Raymond, always on the lookout for a pal to accompany him to the local bar, plus a broad assortment of neighbors who had known Renaud's family all their lives.

Adjustment was the name of the game. I soon realized that if our backgrounds didn't have much in common, neither did our natures. Renaud is calm, logical and methodical. I am impatient, disorganized and impulsive. Renaud is sports-minded; I like plays and concerts, and my good times don't involve two hundred good buddies and a keg of beer.

Religion was not the hurdle we expected it to be. It was easy to promise not to interfere with each other's religious beliefs, since neither of us is inclined to interfere with others' convictions. However, in the long run religion was the only thing we didn't interfere with. Hot on the heels of our smugness in thinking we had everything under control loomed the rest of it, like a snowball rolling downhill, gathering both momentum and volume and threatening to pack us in.

With little time to work out compromises, our complacent little democracy soon showed signs of insurrection. Our strengths and weaknesses surfaced while we struggled to smooth out genetically coded reactions. Often, we took one step forward only to slide two steps back.

Renaud's French Roman Catholic, large-family, country background and voluble social life did not blend noiselessly with my Scottish Protestant, small-family, urban upbringing and subdued social leanings.

I had had no previous experience with cultural differences, so it was an eye-opener to discover that all St. Anicet men, if not all rural men, or all French Canadian men — perhaps all men everywhere — are tied to their place of birth by a short umbilical cord. This meant, of course, that there could never be an objective answer to the question of where we were going to live. By the time I realized Renaud had a five-year plan for maneuvering me into a permanent mooring in St. Anicet, the deed was done and I felt as alien as a quiet clove in a jar of noisy peaches. I'd had the wrong idea about compromise all along.

When I was young, my ideas of marriage were formed along the lines of: settle down, get job, buy house, raise children, retire. It was not exactly the pattern Renaud had his heart set on. For one thing, job, to me, was simply work for pay. Not so for Renaud, who had no desire to go through life working for someone else.

The first inkling I had that Renaud cherished a burning ambition to start his own business and become independently poor, was on a Sunday afternoon in the first springtime of our marriage. Steam swirled up from the melting snow in our driveway. As we wiped mud spatters off our grey Pontiac Renaud asked, "What would you say if I quit my job and went into business on my own?"

Without missing a beat in my swoosh of suds over rear fender, I said, "Sure."

A few days later Renaud, watching me peel potatoes at the kitchen sink, said, "Uuuuhhhh . . ."

"Yes?" I asked.

"I've been thinking about going into contracting," Renaud said casually. "You know, roads, paving, excavation . . ." He sat down at the table and fussed with the placemats, knives and forks.

I shrugged. "Why don't you then?" I plopped the pot of potatoes on the burner, turned it on and started the coffee. Renaud looked doubtful, said that it would be a long while before we could make enough to live on and reminded me that we didn't have any capital.

A few days later, as we left the office at lunchtime, Renaud brought up the subject again. He cleared his throat, coughed and said, "What if I quit my job, borrowed some money and — uh — went into business?"

"I already told you," I said easily. "It's O.K. with me."

"I know you said that," said Renaud. "But I would have to set up the business in St. Anicet. I can buy a piece of the farm near the gravel pit. But the hours would be long. I wouldn't get home very much."

"I understand," I said.

"Weelll . . ." said Renaud a week later.

"Well, what?" I asked.

"I've done it!" he said exuberantly.

"Done what?" I asked.

"Quit my job!"

"Sure," I said, not believing him.

"I really did," said Renaud. "By next week we'll be in business."

And we were.

We borrowed money from Household Finance to buy an old truck and a small paving roller. We were in business. And in debt. Renaud thrust himself headlong into the world of construction, coming home late, exhausted, dirty and, if not always smiling, at least fulfilled.

It was a successful summer, but with November and cold weather came unemployment, and another decision — to take a vacation in Florida.

We gave up our rented home, sold half the furniture, stored the rest and bought a second-hand travel trailer as a springboard to our second honeymoon.

Nerves jangling from our first construction season, we were optimistic about this carefree trip, but the producers of the classic honeymoon movie *The Long, Long Trailer* wouldn't have been inspired. "Carefree" was hardly the word for it. Neither was "honeymoon." We didn't know the first thing about trailer life. Not about backing up, attaching the electrical system, operating the hitch or living squashed into an uncongenial six-by-eight-foot space that seemed no larger than a walk-in closet.

The first day out we forgot about the trailer when backing up at a gas station and splintered a hole in the side. It was an apt beginning to a trip that became an education in marriage and compromise.

Part of the problem was the trailer itself. It was not a sleek, lightweight, factory-built dream home on wheels. It was heavy, clumsy and made of plywood. It was also painted a conspicuous red. With the diminishing silhouette of a lying-down tear-drop, starting about five feet from the ground in front and curving down to a point at the rear, it was so low that anyone over four feet, six inches tall couldn't stand in it. After hitting his head on the low door frame twice, Renaud learned to duck in time. I never got the hang of it. I cleaned house by crawling on my hands and knees and sweeping the floor with a whisk broom.

There were times when "Little Red" looked like a cosy haven of red and white gingham curtains, varnished plywood and romantically dim lighting. But the lighting was romantic only if we didn't have to see what we were doing and no matter how it looked, it always smelled like mildew and mothballs.

We were novices, so everything we accomplished without hurting ourselves, the trailer or the car was a victory — though not always a step forward.

Not knowing about trailer parks, we camped at garages, even off the side of the road. When we finally got to Miami Beach, we set up camp in a beautiful picnic area on the ocean. It had everything — washrooms, fireplaces and garbage cans. I even did a little laundry, hanging it on a rope strung between two palm trees. But we couldn't understand how come we were the only campers taking advantage of such great facilities. We watched the surf chewing at the beach and the palms swishing in the breeze, then went in to bed — where we stayed until around midnight, when stern knuckles at the end of the long arm of the law knocked on our short red door, and a voice barked, "move along."

We had settled into a municipal park, not a free camp ground.

Hitching the trailer, we drove off in our pyjamas and found a vacancy at Howard's Trailer Park on Biscayne Boulevard, just when the Florida skies opened up to answer the combined prayers of all the tomato farmers in the state. It rained for days. Our teardrop seemed to shrink. Renaud and I got in each other's way and on each other's nerves, bickering and quarrelling in boredom and hot, damp discomfort, which reduced us to such intelligences as "What do you want to do?"

"What do you mean, what do *I* want to do?"

"Well, why should *I* always be the one to make decisions around here?"

"Huh, who's idea was *this* anyway?"

"Not *mine*, you can bet on that!"

"Well it sure wasn't *mine*!"

"Oh yeah?"

"Yeah!"

To make matters worse, we both sulked. Renaud often sat in the humid little trailer, looking sad and feeling sorry for himself. I stalked off to sit in the back seat of the Pontiac, muttering terrible things about insensitive husbands and Florida certainly not being all it was cracked up to be, while wondering how to get back in the trailer for the night without losing my pride.

Finally, the sun came out. Heat waves wafted up from our patio and hovered over the hibiscus bordering the trailer park. We were in love again, smiling at each other and at neighboring trailerites in their shiny, factory-built homes. We swam in the ocean, visited Parrot Jungle, hunted for seashells and made a half-hearted attempt to get to Key West. Then, while touring a minor back road, the car quit and we had to spend an entire hot, dusty afternoon in the immediate proximity of the obscene activities of an exhibionist chimpanzee chained to a tree at a run-down garage, where we waited for parts to be sent from a town that was three hours away.

By mid-December, homesick and nearly broke, we headed for home. The newly regenerated-by-sunshine honeymoon atmosphere faded abruptly as we headed back to the Canadian winter. It didn't help that we had bought two heavy bags of oranges to distribute back home — as the weather got colder and we spent our dwindling resources on motels at night, we had to drag the ungainly bags into our rooms so they wouldn't freeze.

"You *had* to have oranges."

"*I* had to have oranges? It wasn't *my* idea to buy oranges."

"That's it — blame it on me . . ."

There was little joy in returning to no house, no job and no prospects, with Christmas just around the corner and most of the winter yet to get through.

* * * * ○ * * * *

CHAPTER 2

It's Our Move

Broke, jobless and homeless, but nicely tanned, we arrived in Montreal in a snowstorm, rented an unfurnished apartment in the north-end suburbs and got jobs. I went to work for Reader's Digest; Renaud worked as a salesman for a heavy equipment company.

Our scrounged-up, cast-off furnishings included, for a bed, an ancient fold-down divan whose legs collapsed as often as possible. We kept our clothes in cardboard boxes and ate off the kitchen counter standing up, because we didn't even have chairs.

Everything was fine until I got sick one morning, and stayed sick, all day, every day. I not only couldn't stand the smell of food or cigarette smoke, but had a hard time tolerating fresh air. I complained to Renaud that all day long everyone in our building cooked cabbage and sausage spiced with garlic. He felt sorry for me and put his arm comfortingly around my shoulders. He even brought me dry crackers and black tea in the morning, but I stayed sick. I wore a path to the bathroom and threw up so often I had to set a chair in front of the toilet. I even fainted a couple of times. I was far too sick to go to a doctor.

"I wonder," I said weakly, as I curled up on the wobbly divan beside Renaud one evening after this had gone on for a couple of weeks. "It's lasting too long for flu. You don't suppose I could be pregnant, do you?"

"Of course you are," Renaud said, adding sagely, "Why do you think you've been having morning sickness?"

"Is that what this is?" I asked. "I thought morning sickness just lasted mornings."

Apparently I was the last to know, because nowhere did my delighted bombshell of news meet with so much as a flicker of surprise — except from the landlord.

We found a two-room basement flat in the east-end suburbs. It was wonderful to step out of the sweltering heat of the summer city into the cave-like coolness of our new home, with the odor of fresh paint clinging to the bright walls. Fresh paint was better, by far, than cabbage, sausage and garlic.

Broke as we were, Renaud borrowed $400.00 and invested in a piece of swampland on the shores of Lake St. Francis, a mile east of St. Anicet. Early the following Sunday, we drove west along the lakeshore. After coasting over a small rise and rounding a curve, we pulled over on the gravel shoulder facing a long, scooped-out bay protected on the left by a south arm that was the village of St. Anicet, and on the right by a north arm, where puffs of water willows padded the shoreline, punctuated by a neat row of Lombardy poplars. The water of the bay stretched from arm to arm in a smooth, satin ripple, decorated with lily pads, frosted with lilies and garnished by a clear sun simmering a light mist away. Clearly visible from where we were, tucked between the willows and poplars of the north arm of the bay, stood the old field-stone homestead built by Renaud's ancestor, Jean-Baptiste LeBeau-dit-Caza.

Our little piece of St. Anicet swampland was to the east,

at the bottom of the bay (in more ways than one), between the two protective arms and facing the broadening lake and the St. Lawrence River.

"What do you think?" Renaud asked, leaping from the car and coming around to help me.

"Ummm, nice," I said, lumbering out of the car, and stirring up clouds of mosquitoes as I picked my unwieldly, first-pregnancy way through the underbrush.

I was disappointed. Not that I had expected a mowed lawn and rose bushes, but I didn't expect our property to be almost under water. Nausea, however, encouraged reflection rather than comment, and I looked dully at our bit of real estate, wondering what Renaud had in mind.

Evidently he was more forward-thinking than I because he was almost ecstatic. "Look at these trees!" he exulted. "Look at that lake! Just look at that view!" and "Isn't it wonderful to have a place on the water?"

"*On* the water?" I asked myself. "I'm sure it is," I said aloud, grabbing his arm for support and pulling my good suede shoe out of a mud hole. So what if the bay was lovely. What could we possibly do with this little piece of swamp that was ours? Ours also were three huge water willows, a couple of maple trees and about five million cattails.

Renaud took my hand in his and smiled down at me. "Isn't it great!" he enthused.

"Huummm," I said. "Oh, yes. Very nice. Just fine."

"Look," said Renaud. "Over there we can make a little pier into the bay and maybe get a boat. In fact," he continued, "nothing stops us from building a cottage right away."

Leaving me on a mound of high ground (about three inches above the mud), he picked his way through the cattails, pacing off the property and sight-spotting where our dream cottage should be built.

"We could start slowly," he said, "haul in some fill to raise the land, build the cottage, and by next summer, come down for weekends and fix it up inside a little bit at a time."

Raise the land? Umm, yes I suppose . . . Influenced by the nesting instinct that makes women long for their own place, however small, I began warming to this idea. I shut my eyes and imagined cedar hedges, currant bushes and clumps of iris where the cattails grew. I also imagined a tidy cottage with Swiss lace curtains, pine cupboards and braided rugs.

For the rest of the summer Renaud worked in Montreal during the week and in St. Anicet for his construction business evenings and weekends. He cleared and filled our lot and started building. We were thrilled with life. It was 1954, and here we were, married just two years and we owned our own business, were building our first new home and now we were going to be a real family. Renaud hired men to mix and pour cement to cast the six-inch concrete slab floor in our cottage. They cast blocks for the walls, covering them with burlap and keeping them wetted down to cure. The single partition down half the center of the twenty-by-twenty-two-foot cottage — in fact, all the walls — were concrete block, a good thirteen inches thick and uninsulated.

We were thrilled at the prospect of owning our own place. It was far from the rush, soot and noise of the summer city. I looked forward to having our own summer retreat. Ah, the freedom of the wilderness, the peace of the countryside, the gentle elements, the tranquil pace. Tranquil? A lot *I* knew!

Winter came, and in January 1955 Billy was born. Nothing could have made us happier. But there was work to be done. Most of it by ourselves and a great deal of it by whoever we could get to help us. By April the cottage was finished. The outside walls were stuccoed and the inside walls were cov-

15

ered with the cheapest thing we could find, ten-test. It looked like pressed oatmeal and resisted every attempt to brighten the place by soaking up gallons of sizing and paint.

Later we papered the walls, but the paper shrank, curled and peeled. Much later we did what we should have done in the first place — put up wood panelling.

When we drove out in spring, I was glad to see that the cattails were gone, that the lake ice had almost disappeared and that the sun was shining on the cottage's brand-new white stucco walls. There was still a lot of mud though, and twisted heaps of scrap lumber lay among broken concrete blocks. Sawdust, gravel, nails and torn shingles were strewn about. Dollops of hardened cement relaxed against the foundation, and the tree closest to the building sported a glaring wound twelve inches across. I also saw for the first time that the roofers had used bright blue shingles ("It's what they had, so it's what they used," said Renaud). When the painters came, they decided to be original about the color scheme. They painted the wooden upper portion of the cottage in stripes: one board red, one board white, Renaud shrugged. "It's what they had," he said, "so it's what they used."

Meanwhile, back in our basement flat in the city, we noticed that what had at first seemed so cool — so delightful — was no longer delightful, and much moister than it should have been.

CHAPTER 3

* * * * ○ * * * *

Look at All the Money We'll Save!

" *How come* it's rusty?" Renaud asked, peering curiously at his dinner knife. Later he asked, "Say — how come my Sunday shoes have powdery green stuff all over them? They were all right last week." And still later, "Whew! Does this closet ever *smell!*"

About the same time that the mildew appeared, black, tar-like stuff started oozing up between the floor tiles. It stuck to our shoes and tracked all over the apartment. The only thing that would budge the stuff was lighter fluid. But lighter fluid compounded the problem by melting the maroon and green asphalt tiles.

We were good sports about the mildewing, tarry apartment all winter — even after Billy was born. Then one evening in April we came home to no electricity and two inches of water on the floor. We had no choice but to take off our shoes and socks and wade to bed in bare feet. Spring thaw had entered our basement flat. It was the last straw.

In May we found a second-floor apartment a few miles west, in the suburbs. We were dry again, but we couldn't afford anything. We bought paper window-shades for the bedrooms, but had no curtains anywhere. I polished the hardwood floors by applying paste wax, putting little Billy in a cardboard box with an old blanket under it, tying a rope around the box and hauling him back and forth until the floor shone.

With Renaud's sales bonus points from work, we ordered a bed, a coffee table, a cedar chest and a dreadful chrome and red plastic kitchen set. We also had an old crib for Billy, an old black and white TV set, an old red damask sofa and chair set and an ancient wringer washing machine that threw me across the kitchen every time I reached inside and touched the sink at the same time.

But it was an upstairs apartment and there was no yard, no park nearby and no place for a clothesline. As soon as our one-year lease was up, we rented another upstairs flat a few miles farther west, in Châteauguay. The landlord and his wife (Peter and Nancy) lived downstairs, were also young and had two children. Nancy was the sort of neighbor everybody should have; she showed me how to bake bread, make cabbage rolls and borscht and knit socks.

We were in Châteauguay about a year when a sudden attack of nausea overcame me while Nancy and I were having coffee in the hot sunshine of the downstairs porch while our children played in the sand box. I brought Billy upstairs, put him in his crib for his nap, and crawled into bed for the rest of the afternoon. "I'll feel better tomorrow," I told myself.

But the next morning I was still feeling rotten. Sort of seasick. Sunstroke, I thought miserably, pulling the sheet up over my head and shutting my eyes again. Renaud smiled, said, "You do know you're pregnant, don't you?" kissed me goodbye and left for work. The doctor agreed. I was pregnant.

Eight months later, Renaud, who was independent-bound again, brought his new yellow pick-up truck home for me to admire — a certain invitation to the onset of labor. At two in the morning we piled into the cab of the truck with Billy — face flushed with sleep, head of blond curls nodding, tucked between us in his blue blanket. Renaud and I were swamped with love for our little family.

When Joey arrived, we looked for a larger home. Renaud said that it would be nice if we moved a little closer to the business — which needed his undivided attention sixteen hours a day. He was waking up at 4:00 A.M. to go to work and pulling into the driveway for supper at 10:00 P.M., six days a week. When he made this latest announcement, I realized, not for the first time, that every move we made was a shuffle, jump or leap in a westward direction. Toward St. Anicet. Toward the business and where Renaud's roots were.

In October we found a treasure of a house on the outskirts of a small town about twenty miles west, complete with fieldstone fireplace, basement laundry room, garage and landscaped grounds. Guest quarters over the garage, enormous cedar-lined closets and two small work rooms were wonderful bonuses.

I loved the spaciousness of the new house. Renaud was happy with it, too, but made no comment to reinforce my raptures about living here forever. His mind was twenty-five miles farther west; in St. Anicet.

We arranged furniture and polished floors, and for the only time in my life before or since, I had enough storage space.

Within six months, the owner of the house told us that he was moving back to town and needed his house. There we were, with two kids and winter coming, looking for a place to live.

We spent the winter in a cold little bungalow five miles away (to the west, of course), where we had two closets and a kitchen so small it could be washed down with a teacup of water.

Then one stormy Saturday in April, Renaud went out after breakfast and came home with an armful of newspapers, and we began house hunting again. I made a pot of coffee in the cold kitchen as the boys played construction in the bedroom.

Then Renaud and I sat at the table leafing half-heartedly through the "Houses for Rent."

After saying nothing for fifteen minutes, Renaud looked up from the paper, cleared his throat a few times (which should have been a warning) and said, "Let's move to the cottage."

"The cottage!" I exclaimed. "Why, that's just a living room and kitchen. The floor is concrete; there's no heating system and no insulation. That's worse than here!"

"I know," Renaud agreed. "But we could insulate, get an oil furnace, add a couple of rooms and cover the floors."

"There's not even a bathroom!" I exclaimed.

"We'll put one in," Renaud said, looking anxiously across the table at me. "It's not perfect," he said, then added, sounding logical, as usual, "But with no rent to pay it would help us get on our financial feet."

"Yes," I said. "But . . ."

"And don't forget," he interrupted, as though shooting the bolt on his best argument, "it would be closer to the business."

Already out of my depth as a wife, mother and quasi business partner, I was daunted by the idea of settling down where Renaud knew everyone and their language was his, and I knew nobody and understood nothing. So I said, "You mean we would be living in St. Anicet all the time?"

"It's beautiful there," Renaud said.

"Yes, but . . ."

He interrupted again, "You'll *love* it!"

Right in the middle of home hive, I mused. The last twenty miles west. This was beginning to look less and less like sudden inspiration and more and more like long-range planning.

Renaud flattened a grocery bag and happily scribbled a series of numbers on it to show me how much better off we would be as homeowners instead of tenants. "Just look at all the money we'll save!" he exclaimed. "And of course," he reassured me smoothly, "after a few years we'll use it as a cottage again and buy or build a really great house."

Apparently we were destined to end up in St. Anicet anyway, no matter how many moves it took, so I nodded slowly and agreed.

Once the decision was made, it didn't take long for me to get into the spirit of things. I could see Renaud's logic. Closer to the business, no rent to pay, our own home, no summer commute. It was the sensible thing to do. It was even starting to sound rather charming. By the time the sun went down, I was so eager to get started I was rounding up empty boxes, making lists and packing.

On May 1st, moving day, we loaded everything big into our dump truck and filled the car with loose blankets, sheets, clothing and pillows, stuffed in around the two boys, and followed the truck, driven by Renaud's brother Yves, west along Highway 132.

Halfway to St. Anicet, as the truck careened around a sharp curve in Ste. Barbe, two bureau drawers and their contents flew off the truck and skittered across the highway into a plowed cornfield. The truck kept on going, so we stopped and ran into the field, picking up what we could find of our belongings. I carried the drawers on my lap the rest of the way to St. Anicet.

At the cottage we unloaded the car and truck and forced everything into the crowded cottage, where it all remained, piled in mournful heaps for three weeks while we sorted bad from worse, kept bad and threw worse away. Of course, there was the added challenge of not yet having running water. Or electricity.

In short, the place was a mess — inside and out. As soon as the truck and car were unloaded, Renaud kissed me goodbye, waved cheerfully and went off to work. Life was sweet; finally, his home and family were in St. Anicet.

CHAPTER 4

* * * * ○ * * * *

We'll Get Used to It

I used to think that being married was like being queen of a private kingdom. The castle was kept tidy by some sort of magic, the subjects were polite and obedient, and there were no problems that couldn't be solved easily. In other words, I didn't really think at all.

Nor did I dwell on the fact that, romance aside, marriage also meant that two very different people were going to be living together and deciding, sometimes not together, what to do with their time, their money, their energy and their bad habits.

What had happened to the calm, ordered life I expected? I thought back six years to the joy in Renaud's eyes when he saw me getting off the plane from Greenland. I thought back to our wedding, to the pride in his eyes at the births of our two sons. I remembered the enthusiasm when he quit his job to start his own business.

It was May. We had been in the cottage a month. It was not what I had imagined married life to be. My world was small and my outlook smaller. For one thing, there was never time anymore: no time to talk; no time to be just a man and woman in love.

Every afternoon I put Joey in bed for his nap while Billy

sat at the kitchen table coloring his Donald Duck book. Then I picked up a bucket and went down to the lake for water. In my new life in the country, everything revolved around getting water, cleaning up mud and sand, washing diapers in buckets and cooking meals on a gas camp stove. The only thing we did as a couple anymore was disagree about money. What had gone wrong?

One afternoon after settling the boys down, I made a cup of coffee and took advantage of the quiet to sit back and reflect about the past, and wonder about the future. I used to think of marriage as a goal — a fulfillment in itself. Like in so many movies and books that end: " . . . and they lived happily ever after," followed by a gentle fade-out. I never really wondered what "ever after" brought with it, but I sure didn't think it was scrub-boards, chapped hands, an oil lamp and a husband who, although still devoted, loving and caring, was worn down to the socks with financial responsibilities.

All kinds of barbed wire and water hazards were sprouting up in this fragile marriage. For instance, the last thing I would have thought of as a hurdle was funerals. I mean, nobody came up to me before marriage and said, "Now don't forget dear, you're going to have to buckle down and get used to country funerals."

Until we got married, I had never attended a funeral in my young, sheltered life. I soon found out that, implicit in marrying into a large, friendly family from a thriving farm community, was the fact of being related to, and friend, neighbor, business associate and nodding acquaintance to, a lot of people — thus necessitating attendance at a lot of funerals. Suddenly my quaking, sympathetic, well-intentioned self had to make peace with the duration and tenor of the social side of death.

A funeral in the area often turned out to be a drawing card for all sorts of distant and not-so-distant relatives and friends — closé and otherwise. Sad as the loss might be, it was likely to become a full-scale family reunion, followed by the almost picnic atmosphere of a grand luncheon catered by friends and/or local organizations at the parish hall.

At first the almost jovial, public air of funerals horrified me, but as Renaud explained in his gentle way of setting me straight about the bumps of country living, "Many relatives and friends come from far away to attend funerals. It's only natural for them to want to get together as a family, and you'll have to admit it isn't the time to impose directly on the family of the bereaved."

Having me as a wife certainly put Renaud in the role of schoolmaster. I knew nothing about living in the country, dying in the country, raising kids, cooking or managing a household anywhere. I knew how to type business letters, how to hail a taxi and how to rinse out my nylons at the bathroom sink. Such talents were of little value in the context of my new life, which included an exhausted husband who flew out the door every morning in a Dagwood dash and returned to me every evening with shoulders in a bone-weary droop, knees bent and feet dragging. I was having a hard time adjusting to a life that included no close neighbors, no phone, no power and water that came in jugs and buckets. So what the heck was all that earlier big deal that went something like "Oh my goodness, we're not of the same religion?"

There were a lot more bothersome things to get used to — including the new, less tolerant me that emerged in response to my new life.

* * * * ○ * * * *

CHAPTER 5

Local Talent

Life in our city apartment, where there was a landlord to complain to, was not like life in our country cottage.

The cottage was floor (concrete), walls (concrete and ten-test) and roof (bright blue and leaky). It was shelter, but it was far from being the cosy pine and Swiss lace I had dreamed of, and I soon learned that no amount of sweat can atone for incompetence. A job badly done, especially when it is in evidence daily, is still a job badly done, no matter how good the intentions, how much we saved by trying to do it ourselves or how much it eventually cost to get outside help.

Renaud didn't exactly trust my skills when I tackled home repairs, but his admonitions fell on deaf ears in view of his own lapses. Inept as I was, he was no better. He had no problems building a road or dredging a canal, but he was relatively helpless when it came to wielding a paint brush.

We weren't alone in our incompetence. Renaud's favorite and least productive bent was the hiring of local talent, and the stream of workers he directed to our front door were, however eager and willing, often no more able than we were — just less personally involved. They didn't have to live with their mistakes.

Because there was so little money, we could tackle only

one need at a time. We had to have priorities. I could see renovations and repairs stretching off into the distance, disrupting our lives forever. What's more, it would all have to be done as we could afford it and while we were living right there — underfoot.

The most pressing projects were, of course, plumbing and electricity, which launched my first run-in with Renaud's cast of characters.

I met Rosie Lecapable, who came highly recommended by Renaud, on a Sunday afternoon. He was the personification of the expression "old codger." Fragile and stoop-shouldered, with longish hair, grey stubble of beard, rheumy eyes, weathered, sun-browned skin and a bashful smile, Rosie walked with a funny, bouncing shuffle, wore seriously baggy overalls and a faded plaid shirt.

Renaud, Rosie and I crowded into the doorway of the broom closet that was to become our bathroom. It was full of pails, mops, tools, scrub-board, brooms and even an unopened bag of cement. It was too small for a tub or shower, but under the rustic circumstances, "powder room" didn't come to mind either.

Rosie broke the glum silence. "You're gonna need some holes drilled in da floor here, so da water from da pump can drain tro' instead a' soakin' inta da floor," he said breathlessly, pointing to the corner.

"Why should we need a drain hole for the pump?" I protested. "It's a new pump, isn't it?"

Rosie, clearly amazed at my stupidity, looked at Renuad and said, "She don't know dat all pumps drip . . .?"

Right then and there I had my doubts about Rosie. When he left, and while Renaud and I cleared the stuff out of the closet to prepare it for the new sink and toilet that Robidoux Building Supplies had delivered, I spoke up. "Renaud," I began, "don't you think we should hire a real plumber?"

26

"Rosie's real enough," said Renaud. "Don't worry. He knows what he's doing."

"Don't you think he's a little old for this sort of work?" I asked.

"Ah," said Renaud. "That shows he's had experience. You can't beat experience."

"But is he strong enough?" I asked.

"Of course he is," said Renaud, going on to explain other advantages of hiring local talent. "Out here in the country," he said, "you don't have to hire one man to lift the stone and another to dig under it, and one man to hold the pipe and another to measure it."

"But Renaud . . ." I said.

"In the country, Margie," Renaud interrupted, pulling the bag of cement out of the closet and dragging it across the kitchen to the door, ". . . in the country you hire one man and he takes care of the entire job, repairing things as he goes along, replacing baseboards and sweeping up the sawdust."

"How about the plumbing itself?" I asked. "After all, he's not really a plumber, is he?"

"I told you. Don't worry. Rosie can do it."

"Even the pump?"

"Even the pump."

"But how can you be sure?"

"I asked him. He said he could do anything."

It was a good story. Perhaps he was right. After all, he knew Rosie and I didn't. We needed a bathroom, and apparently it was either let Rosie get on with it, or buy a johnny-on-the-spot. I agreed.

Renaud left for work early the next morning just as Rosie arrived. Rosie smiled, took a pick and shovel from the trunk of his old car, and started digging a hole at the base of the outside wall of the bathroom.

I knew nothing about tile fields, crushed rock, cutting

holes in concrete block or being patient while Rosie sat on a rock in the shade at intervals for a smoke. As the days wore on, the slow, methodical sound of Rosie's pick on the stone where the septic tank would be, grated on my nerves.

"When's it going to be *finished*?" I gritted at Renaud on the eve of the fourth day as we looked in the broom closet, where nothing had changed except for the toilet bowl lying on the floor and the sink propped against the wall.

"Don't worry," said Renaud. "I told you, Rosie knows what he's doing. Just leave him alone, and he'll get it done at his own speed."

"Sure," I muttered uncharitably. "Like a small snail digging the Grand Canyon." And Rosie continued to come every morning and dig precise amounts with his shovel, placing measured mounds of dirt neatly along the edge of the excavation. It was plain that he was neither nervous nor in any great hurry.

Living in the country was not so much gosh-darn fun as I'd been led to believe by a certain husband who was out there in the business world carving out a career for himself while I took care of dirty dishes, laundry, hair shampooing, bathing, cooking and cleaning up without a handy, operating water spigot.

Meanwhile, Renaud dragged home drinking water in gallon jugs and I used weedy water dipped with deep resentment from the lake for everything else.

Renaud, away from home most of the time, and with enough business problems to keep him insulated from my world, remained beautifully calm and understanding about the plumbing delays, until the inside work got under way. Then even he had to admit that, diligent as our Rosie was, he had surely never installed a bathroom before in his life. A privy, perhaps, but a bathroom? Never.

Sometimes I tried to speed things up, but Rosie wasn't the

sort to be pressured. Looking dreamily up at the ceiling (or sky), he bounced, shuffled, side-stepped, scratched his beard and whispered, "Won't be long now, Ma'am . . ."

Rosie poked, fitted, lifted, shifted, cut, shovelled and grunted, calling Renaud in for major and minor emergencies and consultation along the way. "Hey — what d'ya tink a dis . . .?" he asked, puzzling over which fittings belonged to the sink and which belonged to the toilet. "Should dat pipe go dis way or dat way?"

Renaud's contributions to these efforts just proved that two wrongs don't make a right, but in spite of both of them, by eight o'clock in the evening of the tenth day, for heaven's sake, they declared the job done, flushed the toilet, threw their arms around each other and went to the kitchen in search of a beer.

While they were celebrating, I went to see how the new bathroom looked and found that there were even leftover pieces, including a heavy copper ring with important-looking perforations. The new sink had a two-by-six-inch chunk removed from the rim with the final turn of the wrench. The baseboards had not been replaced. Sawdust and other debris remained strewn on the floor and the toilet tank was cracked and wobbly, listing to one side. But at this point, who could complain? We had a bathroom.

What we still didn't have was a well. Water for the bath-room was pumped in from the lake. That was fine for the rest of the summer, but when that first country winter caught us early and unprepared, Renaud had to bring home not only the drinking water, but all the household water — this time in five-gallon milk cans — daily. For the entire winter. The water pipe leading to the lake stopped where the water was shallow and, of course, froze solid when the lake did. It froze the following winter, too, in spite of the fact that Renaud's well-meaning brother Maurice said, "Sonofabitch, I can fix that!" and dumped quantities of hay and straw from his barn over the first layer of ice to prevent the freeze from reaching the pipe.

Making those five-gallon cans of water last with all the water tasks in a household with small children (one in diapers) was a humbling experience. I soon found out, whenever water ran short, how much snow had to be melted to make a skimpy pail of water for flushing the toilet.

In spring, when the lake ice melted, the water ran from the lake to the house again. But our joy was short-lived, because the water was stained tobacco yellow from the hay and straw and made the whole house smell remarkably like a stable.

CHAPTER 6

* * * * * ○ * * * *

My Mother Didn't Have No Damn Fool Cupboards in Her *Kitchen*

My second run-in with local talent was when Renaud brought home Mr. Saitfaire to add two bedrooms and a larger bathroom, with a tub.

Mr. Saitfaire's chief characteristic was his undisguised contempt for women. At the first hint of interference from me (I said, "Pleased to meet you"), he looked suspiciously at me and announced to Renaud, "Wimmen don't know nawthing about building."

He got the job, but he had a disconcerting habit of dropping everything whenever a decision had to be made and waiting for Renaud. Or just going home.

I wanted the bathroom to be between the two new bedrooms, with a door to it from either side. Clearly Mr. Saitfaire had never heard of such an outrageous idea. He rolled his eyes round toward Renaud, dug in his heels and said, "I don't take orders from no wimmen!"

Eventually Renaud backed me up about the two doors to the bathroom. He backed me up about deep windowsills, too, and about kitchen cupboards — even though Mr. Saitfaire said, "My mother didn't have no damn fool cupboards in *her* kitchen."

31

Renaud did not back me up about closets, though. I wanted a lot of them; he thought that two small ones in the whole house would be enough. He must have been taking lessons from Mr. Saitfaire, because he said, "My mother didn't have any closets in the whole house, and there were eight of us kids."

He didn't back me up about the bookcases I wanted either. The most I could talk him into were floor to ceiling shelves built along two short walls, and I succeeded in doing that only when I sneaked about it, persuading Frank, a really good carpenter from the village (who is usually too busy for our addled projects), to put them in. They were still not enough.

Then came the miracle of electricity. For three years of summers before the cottage became a year-rounder, we used oil lamps and candles. But no matter how high the wick, nothing was adequate to read or work by.

Electricity meant that I could pull a dangling string and flood our rooms with genuine hundred-watt sunshine — even if it did come from a bare bulb hanging from the ceiling in each room. Now I could read at night.

That wasn't all. In rapid succession, an electric hot plate replaced the portable gas camp stove, a toaster made its debut, a wretched second-hand refrigerator replaced the camp ice box and in the evenings I contentedly brewed pots of tea and sat reading under the dangling bulb after the children were in bed.

Then there was the matter of heat. Our first few winters were bitter. We had to supplement the heat from the little gravity-flow oil furnace backed against the wall between the kitchen and living room before we all died of exposure right there in the house. We decided on the carefree convenience of electric heat.

While I'll freely admit that electric heat has been carefree, the admission itself was the only part of it that was free, as we found out after our first hydro bill. Of course, other culprits were making their presence felt at the monthly meter reading. Since we now thought we had unlimited electricity, we got a hot water tank with heater and put in a few more electric outlets. Then my parents gave us a clothes dryer for our anniversary — a wonderful gift that meant no more lines of wet clothes dripping and slapping at us from long lines strung through the kitchen and living room.

Suddenly we were tripping circuit breakers and the electrical inspector came and told us that we didn't have all that much electricity. His sense of humor was up to the occasion, because when he told us that our new meter and fuse box could not carry such a power load and we needed a special meter with heavy-duty panel, special main fuses and circuit breakers that would cost a few hundred dollars more, he was laughing and shaking his head at our naïveté.

In spite of everything, however, we persisted in giving our home renovations to the local boys. And the trend continued. Even when we decided that a fireplace would be a charming supplement to our heating system.

Our living room leaned toward the colonial look, with a braided rug and an old wing-back chair salvaged from the waiting room in Renaud's Uncle Euclide's dental office. Renaud and I agreed that it would be nice to gather around the cheery glow of a fireplace on stormy evenings, toasting marshmallows and popping corn with our two sons.

So when Renaud bumped into Lionel at the local watering hole early in June and said, "Say, Lionel, we were thinking about building a fireplace. Can you do that?" Lionel, of course, said, "You bet!" and another local talent crossed our threshold.

Lionel came the first week in July and ripped out the north wall of our living room. While he worked quickly with

33

crowbar and hammer to break up the concrete block wall and prepare the foundation, Lionel soon lost momentum. For the rest of the summer, we lived with a gaping hole and cement and stone dust as Lionel slowly and carefully chose each fieldstone for its exact right effect of texture, color and shape before cementing it painstakingly into place. Lionel's specifications were so exacting that he sometimes took all day to choose and install one stone. Though he proudly summoned me to drop whatever I was doing, whether it was laundry or going to the bathroom, to applaud each stone placement before he went off to celebrate, I was hard-pressed not to openly rebel as Mother Nature's wild creatures made their way into the house through the three-by-four-foot hole in the living room wall.

To make matters worse, something was building a nest on the ivy planter in the kitchen with the obvious intention of starting a family, and one morning I found a bat hanging upsidedown from the drapery track in the living room.

By the time good ol' Lionel started on the fourth row of stone, his working day and my fuse became much shorter, and Lionel's sojourns at the local watering hole became alarmingly frequent.

As August merged into September, then October, even Renaud rebelled. He told Lionel to get the job finished before winter set in.

Lionel, shaken by this abrupt change in attitude, said that he couldn't do a good job if he had to do it fast, and suggested that we board off the hole, stuff burlap in the cracks, and let him finish next spring.

Renaud, who, as a rule, speaks with rare patience, bewildered Lionel by putting his foot down.

"But there isn't time to line up enough fieldstone now . . ." protested Lionel.

"Then use brick," said Renaud tersely.

"But it's already started with fieldstone," said Lionel with disbelief.

"Use brick!" Renaud commanded.

"It'll look funny," whined Lionel.

"Brick," said Renaud.

"But . . ." said Lionel.

"Finish it!" said Renaud.

And he did.

The idea of a fireplace proved to be impractical, though, because with no basement, no shed and no garage, there was no place to keep firewood except piled up against the fieldstone and brick chimney outside, where it froze solid for the winter with the first storm of the season.

* * * * ○ * * * *

CHAPTER 7

After All, What Could Possibly Go Wrong?

Another disadvantage of moving to the cottage was the concrete floors. They were tolerable when we were there on a summers-only basis, but not year-round. After enduring one winter of frozen feet, Renaud said, "You might as well go to Robidoux's and pick out tiles. And get good ones. We're not going to be putting down new flooring every five minutes."

Taking his word for it, I picked commercial-quality grey tiles in a chip design. It was neutral enough to blend with anything, and tough enough to last for the next fifty years. I needn't have bothered.

Renaud sent over a couple of local talents to lay plywood sheathing on the concrete floor and glue down the tiles. But none of us knew that you were supposed to leave air space between concrete floors and wood. After a while, the humidity rotted the underlay. We tripped over up-curled tiles, knocking them loose and kicking them back into place. When the floor got dirty, I could pick up the distorted tiles, with splintered wood clinging to the backs, scrub them off at the sink and replace them. And it wasn't funny.

When the smell of moldy wood got strong enough, Renaud begged Frank to come and bail us out. Frank ripped the floors apart, shovelled the whole mess out the door, and rebuilt the floor properly, with "sleepers," air space and brand-new supported sheets of flooring plywood. All this took fifteen and a half days, most of it with the floor divided into a gridwork of two-by-twos. With a two-year-old, a four-year-old and now another one on the way, we hopscotched over the gridwork all day, every day. It was like living in an egg crate, but more nervewracking.

That should have discouraged me from trying anything new, but for some nearsighted reason and a yearning to pick our own sun-warmed tomatoes, I planted a garden. Just as it was coming along toward harvest time, the honey-wagon came to empty the septic tank and rolled over my garden on its way in, then sat on it while going about its business.

Then there was the local talent that Renaud sent to clear away dead branches and other debris in early spring, who managed to hack off "dat stubborn big weed, Ma'am . . ." (which just happened to be a three-year-old lilac), rip out three petunias and dig up the chives, rhubarb and lilies of the valley to put in grass seed.

I certainly won't forget handy-man Alex, who set fire to a pile of rubbish five feet from our healthy and producing plum tree, in a high wind aimed at the tree. As I ran for a water bucket, he headed me off, saying reassuringly, "Awwww, it won't make no difference a'tall, Mrs. Caza. It's not going to hurt your tree none. It's *good* for it!" It wasn't.

I don't have good instincts about landscaping. Neither does Renaud, though that never stopped him. About once a year or so I look around and think that the place could look neater. But I complain silently — with good reason, because if I mention it to Renaud he gets a gleam in his eye for law and order in the foliage, rummages around for the rusty saw under the stairway and my good sewing shears and heads for the willow trees, cedars, fruit trees and cranberry bushes, intending to correct the neglect of the entire summer in one afternoon. Sometimes his herbal victims recover; sometimes they never regain their composure — like one enormous weeping willow that once swept gracefully over the lake. He pruned it determinedly until there wasn't a single branch left on the east side of it before stepping back to see his handiwork. Then left it like that.

When Linda arrived to round out our little family in May, 1960, we turned the attic space above the main cottage into another bedroom.

So we were back into construction, with insulation, flooring, windows, built-in chests of drawers, and even, to the horror of Mr. Saitfaire, a door at the end of the south wall of this upstairs room, which led onto the almost-flat roof over the downstairs bedroom wing, giving us a splendid twenty-by-forty-foot sundeck.

It was lovely. But now, of course, we had to put fencing around it for the safety of the children. Renaud shook his head resignedly as he took out his wallet to pay the last of the local talent and hardware bills. "I hope that's all," he said.

But it was worth it. Just look at that sundeck! What a wonderful place for picnics, suntans and sleeping under the stars. Who could ask for more? "Just look at that view, Renaud!" I exclaimed as I stretched my arms upward under the cool shade of the big water willow that draped over the sundeck.

It was a view worth waiting for — gentle breezes, swishing branches, ruffled lake frosted with a shimmer of waxy white and yellow water lilies, sailboats catching brisk winds out near the channel.

"Ah, city people don't know what they're missing," I said to Renaud, who had remained silent throughout my contented soliloquy (proving, ultimately, that he knew more than I did). Happy in the false security of ignorance, I settled back into my lawn chair and appreciated the country life some more. After all, what could possibly go wrong?

CHAPTER 8

* * * * * ○ * * * * *

How Come Nothing Ever Stays Done Around Here?

What could possibly go wrong didn't waste any time. No matter how much we did, there was never a time when everything was finished at once. There were always loose ends somewhere, and some of those loose ends grew other loose ends to trip us up.

We started at one end of the house and worked our way to the other, step by logical step. But by the time we had one thing finished, something else had caved in, peeled off, worn out or in some other way become loathsome. So we shouldn't have been surprised one Sunday, during a summer storm, when the roof over our still-new bedroom wing started leaking.

Torrents of wind-driven rain whipped the branches of the willows and sluiced over the windows. I had just stacked the lunch dishes in the sink when, over the steady pelt of rain on the roof and rain on the windows, we heard a quiet but clear *snick-splat, snick-splat,* coming from the direction of our new bedroom. It was the sound of rain on our recently acquired gold plush rug.

I put a pot under the *snick-splat,* which turned to *pling-twang.* The next morning, Renaud called Mr. Saitfaire, who said it wasn't his fault, but he would come and see if he could help us out.

"It's all right," he assured Renaud after examining the roof.

39

"Of course, it's the railing around that sundeck you know."
An accusing look was sent my way. "I'll send over a couple
of men to caulk around the support posts."

The men came, the men caulked, but when the next storm
came in the night, about two weeks later, the *snick-splat*
nagged us awake as raindrops snuggled into the rug.

Three years, nine sure-fire solutions and as many failures
later, Mr. Saitfaire still maintained that none of it was his
fault. He said he had another idea. He recommended that we
hire him to completely re-roof the sundeck. Renaud told him
to get started, even though I reminded him that if Mr.
Saitfaire couldn't build a leakless roof first time around, how
did he expect him to build one on top of it?

Of course, Mr. Saitfaire put the entire blame for the
problem on "them ideas wimmen get." He intimated that if
women were addled enough to want such an absurd thing as
a sundeck, at least they should have the good judgment to
keep people off it.

The new roof was installed, and I know it made a difference, because the next rain storm also came during the night
and the drips, instead of digging into the rug, found a better
spot — my pillow! The next morning Renaud called Mr.
Saitfaire, and I rearranged the bedroom furniture for the
duration of the rainy season.

There followed another bout of examining and caulking.
Finally Mr. Saitfaire said he'd found the problem and could
fix it. He said we needed an entire new outside wall on the
south end of the upstairs bedroom leading out to the sundeck.

Shortly after the bill was paid, I got out of bed one stormy
midnight and slammed pots onto two wet circles on the rug.
Renaud snored on, oblivious to the snare-drum roll of rain
hitting the metal.

I stuffed a handful of washcloths into the pots to soften the
racket and climbed back into bed, trying to fall asleep by

counting sheep — pacing them with their leaps landing in puddles of water to the soft sound of *splish, splish, splish* . . .

The roof leaked for another ten years. Every spring we had the roof inspected and caulked, but nothing worked. By now the bedroom ceiling was softening and bulging inward and there were two cavities through which water poured when it rained, as though directed through a downspout.

At last Renaud put his foot down and told Mr. Saitfaire that he didn't care how he did it, but he had to fix the roof. He was pretty upset, but Mr. Saitfaire was unperturbed. "Huh, you tink you got a leaky roof?" he snorted. "You just come to *my* place. I'll show you a leaky roof."

That was enough for Renaud. He picked up the phone and called a genuine, honest-to-God roofing contractor, who gave us, finally, a leakless roof.

As the children got older, the house got smaller. Billy, Joey and Linda started school, brought home friends and animals and acquired possessions with the momentum of a runaway downhill bus. We needed more space, so we turned the kitchen window into a door and built a family room overlooking the lake.

I wanted this room to have floor-to-ceiling storage units to make up for having only two closets in the whole house for the five of us. Renaud said no. Mr. Saitfaire looked triumphant.

Like everything else, the new family room was too small. We put the new freezer in there, and a day-bed. Renaud added an artificial orange tree on our anniversary. The children added a pool table, hockey game, electric guitar and amplifier, a desk, lazy-boy chair, stereo, a hamster, an ant farm, a white mouse named Harold, two turtles, two tropical fish, a full-size set of Ludwig drums and a gallon jar of tadpoles.

CHAPTER 9

✳ ✳ ✳ ✳ ○ ✳ ✳ ✳ ✳

The Storms Within

It was 4:00 A.M. when the pipes under the house exploded. As soon as I heard the *click, click, snaaap, sszzzzzz,* I knew that a torrent of icy water was flinging itself all over the frozen earth under the house.

Renaud, sound asleep beside me under a warm heap of quilts, didn't stir. I decided not to wake him. Instead, I got out of bed, went into the bathroom, turned off the pump and went back to bed. When the alarm clock went off would be soon enough to face the battle of the pipes and a husband who might well start wondering what was wrong with the carefree bachelor life. I fell asleep with no trouble at all. I thought I might as well.

When the alarm rang at six, I opened my eyes to a moment of immediate and total recall. The pipes. Ah, yes . . .

The children would wake up any minute. The dog and cat had to be let out and breakfast prepared, water or no water. Life goes on, even on burst-pipe mornings. I pushed the mound of quilts next to me and said, in a whisper that might as well have been a shout, "Renaud, the pipes . . . ."

He groaned. "Awww no, not the pipes. Not again . . ."

When the pipes burst, water gushed into the earthen crawl space under the house. The crawl space (and whoever coined that phrase wasn't kidding) was about two feet deep, extended the full length and breadth of the bedroom wing and was laced throughout with a local-talent plumber's nightmare of pipes weaving in all directions from under the pump in the bathroom to tub, kitchen sink and outdoor faucet.

To get into the crawl space, you had to go through a trap door located under one of the bunk beds built against the south wall of the boys' room.

Billy and Joey's built-in beds look like a giant chest fourteen feet long, with mattresses at either end over lift-up lids and a raised storage section between.

On burst-pipe mornings we evicted whoever was sleeping in the bed over the trap door, removed his mattress, raised the lift-up lid, removed the boxes of stored boots, skates, broken lamps, tent poles, sleeping bags, picture frames and too-bad-to-use-but-too-good-to-throw-away frying pans. Then the trap door was raised and someone (not me!) had to hang upside-down like a bat over the two-and-a-half-foot-high edge of the built-in bed and stick his head down through the opening to find the trouble while someone else (usually me) held onto the ankles of the hangee to keep him from slithering through head first.

Renaud eased out of bed and headed for the tool drawer. Shivering and muttering crossly, he complained that the flashlight batteries were dead, borrowed my good colonial lamp from the living room and attached an extension cord.

Renaud gave orders, and the rest of us (the children were now up and dressed) jumped to obey.

"Are there any pieces of rug, linoleum, cardboard or old blankets we can throw down on the mud?" he called out hopefully. We scattered, bringing back grocery bags, garbage bags and broken-down cardboard boxes.

Then he called for a "wrench, a hammer, screwdriver, pair of pliers . . . What do you *mean* you don't have a wrench?

You surely don't expect me to rip these pipes apart with my bare hands, do you?" At that point I wouldn't have put it past him, but I had the good sense not to say so.

We lowered him, finally, head first, with lamp, extension cord and tools, through the trap door, and he crawled to the burst pipe, where he hammered, banged and sent up pleas for more co-operation and tools. "Who disconnected the (mutter, mutter) extension cord?" he demanded. And, "How do you expect me to see anything down here with no light?"

I reconnected the extension, then stood above the trap door, waiting to carry out orders instantly. When Renaud called out triumphantly, "O.K., turn the pump on!", I raced cooperatively to the bathroom and threw the switch.

Over the rumbling and gurgling of the pump I didn't hear his bellow to "Shut it off, *quick*!" and by the time I did, it was too late to hope for a dry, good-humored husband that day.

Renaud finally emerged from the crawl space with fervent promises to do something about the pipes before next winter. That's what he always says right after fixing burst pipes, but he always forgets when the pipes stop freezing. So I was surprised one day in spring when he sent an electrician to bolt a heater with thermostat to the floor beam in the crawl space.

The pipes still froze in winter, but not as often. And our electric bill was alarmingly higher. It didn't make sense. After all, we had built the new bedroom wing with winter storms in mind. Every autumn our handyman Alex installed the storm windows, covering them with heavy plastic and banking all around the building with sand and earth. Still, every year, even with the heater, the pipes froze.

Then one day Alex came to repair a section of the outside wall that had been damaged by humidity. He stripped away a four-by-eight panel of sheathing, and there it was. *Nothing*! That devil Saitfaire — he hadn't put an inch of insulation in the whole bedroom wing.

Our water problems didn't end with exploding pipes, though; we also had the battle of the pump. This is a chronic condition known as not enough air space in the top of the tank. We always knew it was time to do something about it when the pump started every half-minute or so, day and night. Like elective surgery, the problem can be stalled indefinitely, but we all knew that the day would come . . .

The way to deal with the pump, we thought, aside from calling one of Renaud's local talents or a real plumber, was to do it ourselves by draining the water out of the tank so that some air could get in. To do that, the plastic pipe joining the pump to the storage tank had to be disconnected and the tank emptied. It was a simple job, except that the disconnector of pipes (again, not me) had to stand out of range as much as possible and brace himself for a powerful shower as the pressure was released.

For the next half-hour or so, someone had to squat in the corner next to the pump, holding a small pot under the pipe from the tank to catch the several gallons of water that drooled out at a maddeningly slow pace until the tank was empty.

It would have been easier if the pipe had not been so close to the floor, because then it could have drained into a pail. As it was, each small pot would be filled with water, then removed and another small pot set in its place while the first was emptied into the tub.

It took patience, because you had to stay on the scene the whole time. No matter how slow the flow of water, walking away and leaving the pot alone merely invited the drooling pipe to speed up and overflow. When the tank was finally empty, the pipes were reunited and, with any luck at all, the pump started working as it was supposed to — until the next episode.

The last time we struggled through this ordeal, there was

a weak hose and/or a weak connecting clip. Renaud finished emptying the tank, and I watched with interest as he connected the plastic pipe, attached the clip, tightened it and turned on the pump. Then he stood up from his cramped position and stretched with relief just as the clip flew off and water shot out in a powerful stream right at his knees. He bent over quickly, shut off the power, straightened up, cast a menacing look my way and muttered a few sullen incoherencies. He went into the bedroom, changed his clothes and started the process all over again.

Finally it was done. This time he tightened the clip extra firmly, examined it, tugged at it and pronounced it satisfactory. Then, peering at it intently to see if there was any sign of weakness, he flipped the switch.

This time it waited a few seconds so it could get up to pressure and then let go just as Renaud, still examining the clip closely, opened his mouth to say, "It seems to be all right now . . ."

He reached for the switch, then stood up, rivulets of water streaming miserably down the enraged contours of his face and turned toward me with a wrench in one hand and a wet bathmat in the other. His look was grim.

There's something endearingly sad, but terribly, terribly funny about a dignified businessman husband standing in wet thermal knits, looking with abject fury at a small pump. I choked back a tactless whoop and retreated just beyond the doorway, ostensibly to get dry towels.

Renaud was drawing a long, quavery breath and starting the whole process again as I peered around the corner from the hallway. This time when he turned the pump on, it didn't wait to gather momentum. It let him have it right away. Enough is enough. The pump would have to be dealt with later — after things cooled down and dried off a bit.

* * * * * ○ * * * *

Two — and More — Solitudes

CHAPTER 10

Neighbors

Our country neighbors weren't stacked above, below and beside us like the neighbors in our crowded apartment building in Montreal, but we certainly got to know them better. It could be argued at times whether that would be trading up or down.

Our city neighbors, in fact, were so anonymous that we didn't get to know the family behind the next partition — let alone the one five miles down the road. Like Papa Épais.

Papa Épais was a tall, angular farmer with a plump and virtuous wife named Adèle, several mongrel dogs, a cow, two geese, a bunch of hens and twelve children ranging in age from two years to twenty-two.

Papa Épais was not a nervous man or he wouldn't have encouraged his fourteen-year-old son Oser's ambition to parachute from the barn roof with an umbrella.

Papa Épais, who was proud of Oser, stood in the farmyard, faded coveralls hanging loosely from his skeletal frame, arms hanging at his sides, chin lax and mouth agape as he gazed up at his son perched on the ridgepole of the barn roof.

"Jump," called Papa Épais eagerly. The boy jumped, the umbrella collapsed and Papa Épais watched solemnly as sonny plummeted to the ground. And in spite of everything, survived.

The fact that Papa Épais was a relaxed sort of person didn't mean that the rest of the community could afford to relax, too. I, for one, learned to drive with white-knuckled caution past Papa Épais's house, which was fairly close to the highway, right next to a ditch thickly overgrown with weeds. Papa Épais's dirty-faced little offspring were in the habit of bedevilling passing motorists by tying a filthy string around a dead cat, hiding in the overgrown ditch and suddenly jerking the cat across the highway, directly in front of approaching traffic. They were often chased and were the cause of many close calls and much hot rubber peeled off screeching tires. But that didn't stop them.

Papa Épais told another son, sixteen-year-old Niaizeau (who was a chip off the old block) to get rid of the swallows nesting up under the eaves inside the barn. Instead of heading for the woods at top speed, Niaizeau, who had an inordinate amount of faith in Papa Épais, studied the birds as they darted into the eaves and swooped out again through the barn door and into the sunlight.

"How we gonna do that, Paw?" he asked, scratching his rear end and shifting his slight weight from one foot to the other.

Arms akimbo, Papa Épais directed Niaizeau to lean a long, unsafe ladder against the barn wall and climb up to where the offending birds were nesting.

Obediently Niaizeau climbed to the top of the ladder, picked up a bird in each hand and stood there, teetering on the top rung.

"Paw," Niaizeau called out. "What'll I do now?"

"Come down the ladder," said Papa Épais.

"How?" asked Niaizeau.

"Put them birds in your pockets," said Papa Épais.

"I got no pockets, Paw," said Niaizeau.

"Well, never mind then," said Papa Épais. "Just come

down the best you can. *But don't let go them birds!*"

Ever obedient, Niaizeau gripped the birds firmly, took a shaky step downward, lost his footing and landed flat out, somewhat the worse for wear, on the barn floor at Papa Épais's feet. Birdless.

Papa Épais raised his family by the land, but he was not particularily good at farming and not at all fond of work. Whenever providence supplied someone to help with the chores, Papa Épais preferred to sit back under the cherry tree between the house and barn and watch a cheaply-come-by hired hand take over his responsibilities.

Papa Épais would see a derelict picking up bottles on the side of the road and offer him a handout to till his field, throwing in a night's sleep or two plus a few home-cooked meals, courtesy of his long-suffering wife Adèle.

One such hired hand, a middle-aged transient, went to work for Papa Épais early one summer and stayed on for the whole season. He was the owner of one piece of well-chewed gum, which he carefully stored, when not in use, in an old, round Dodd's Kidney Pill box.

One Sunday morning he was seen working in Papa Épais's field, carefully turning the manure that had just been spread, with a big garden fork. By mid-afternoon he was still laboring at his task and still near the same spot. A neighbor stopped to ask why he was digging around in the steaming field in the hot sunshine of an August Sunday. He stopped to wipe the sweat from his face with a faded red kerchief and explained simply that he had lost his gum and was looking for it. Found it, too.

Papa Épais's most startling custom was one that locals were used to. But early-rising summer commuters swerved in alarm if they happened to be passing Papa Épais's house when he was saluting the dawn by standing on the front doorstep of his paint-peeled farmhouse, turning proudly in his faded long-johns, taking aim at the rising sun and evacuating his bladder. Tradition had been served.

Adèle had a lot to put up with. There were the children, a couple of wives brought home by the older boys, the livestock, picked-up-farm-hands, and especially, Papa Épais himself. But she was a pious, God-fearing woman, who dealt patiently with her life. This was her lot, and she accepted it. Then again, Papa Épais had his fun side, but it was hard to tell whether Adèle benefited from it, since she was often the target.

For instance, unknown to Adèle, but known to everyone else in the parish (he bragged about it), Papa Épais, the old devil, sometimes went to bed early, before his wife. Then he set the stage for his favorite evening entertainment by tying a thread to the rocking chair at the foot of the bed and attaching the other end of the thread to his big toe. Then he would lie back on the bed, pull up the covers, clasp his hands over his stomach and earnestly compose himself to feign sleep.

After Adèle settled the rest of the household, she went upstairs and crawled wearily into bed. When Papa Épais was sure she was asleep, he moved his toe until the rocking chair creaked back and forth at a good pace. Then he woke her with an urgent shove. "Adèle . . ." he whispered hoarsely, "Adèle, your mother's ghost is back, and she wants you to pray for her."

Whereupon the exhausted but terrified Adèle leaped out of bed, whimpering and trembling with fear, and dutifully knelt to pray, while her ungrateful husband nearly expired with suppressed laughter.

Country life was full to bursting with wonderful characters, who were especially wonderful if you weren't directly involved and didn't have to live with them.

Like the spirited old gentleman known as Le Vieux Bissonnette, who was always willing to lend a helping hand. Le Vieux was a good neighbor, and had the best of intentions. But his judgment was sometimes a bit off, as one neighbor found out when Le Vieux offered to help re-roof the barn. The old man volunteered to stay on the ground and hold the support rope that was slung up and over a roof stanchion, and attached like a harness to the man working on the roof.

The rope had to be secure to the person on the ground, and shifted as the job progressed, in order to take up the slack. Everything went fine until Le Vieux got careless. When the roofer called down that he needed more nails, Le Vieux let go the rope. The farmer, braced away from the suddenly slackened rope, somersaulted down the steeply sloped roof, dropped over the edge and hit the ground like a stone.

This same helpful soul also became the talk of the village one Sunday when he offered to drive a neighbor by horse and buggy to the Chaffée, one of the regular supply boats servicing St. Anicet from Montreal. But they were late, and as the team approached the dock, it was apparent that the boat had just kissed the wharf goodbye.

Le Vieux's passenger stood in the buggy as they sped along the street leading to the wharf. "I've missed the boat," he yelled agitatedly at Le Vieux. "Look at that — there it goes — *I've missed the boat!*"

Le Vieux, a wild gleam in his eyes, told his passenger to hang on, and whipped his team to added effort.

"You ain't missed it yet," he bellowed as they clattered down the worn boards of the wharf. And as they reached the end, horses, buggy, driver and passenger flew off and plunged into the river.

Le Vieux led a full life, which was brought to a close in a typically flamboyant manner. He had always said that he and his wife would die together. Then one day, as the years took their toll, Le Vieux's wife passed away after a short illness. In the custom of the day in deep country, the deceased was laid out at home for the traditional wake. Friends and neighbors came to console the family and to prepare and serve food and coffee to sustain the mourners.

Le Vieux went to the grocery store in the village to put in an order to be delivered to his home. About to leave the store, Le Vieux paused, turned, looked at the grocer, said gruffly, "Double that order," left, jumped into his buggy, drove home, went to bed and simply died.

In the country there were neighbors I only knew about from stories of the old days and those I could see for myself, like Papa Épais. And among those I knew, there were many good neighbors: the postman who did errands for me when I was housebound; the neighbor who came in spring with great sheaths of rhubarb and in fall with baskets of perfect tomatoes; the quiet fisherman who left fresh, cleaned, ready-for-the-pan perch in our doorway; and the understanding souls who took care of the children in emergencies. And then there were new neighbors. Summer neighbors, who built cottages around us and made me feel that, at last, I was not alone.

* * * * ○ * * * *

CHAPTER 11

Rats . . .

We *had other neighbors*, too. Neighbors we weren't eager to be friends with. And they'd been living in the area long before we arrived.

That first autumn, while we were hurrying with storm windows and oil drums, the rodent community around us suddenly realized that they not only had new neighbors, but that these new neighbors were planning on staying for the winter and were going to heat their house.

So they made plans of their own. To them it was Christmas, Thanksgiving and moving day all in one. One night, shortly after the first snow fluttered softly around our country home, the quiet was broken by a faint scurrying sound. I got out of bed, turned on the light and shrieked at a small ball of grey mouse rolling across the floor and under the bed.

I leaped back onto the bed and collected my wits as Renaud, who had not seen the mouse, stirred under his pile of quilts and wondered in a loud voice if I had taken leave of my senses.

I explained the situation, perhaps not too coherently, then asked in a trembling voice what he intended to do about it. I mean, you can't just forget about it and go back to sleep when you know there's a mouse right there in the same room with you — under your bed.

Apparently Renaud could. He mumbled calmly, "It's just a mouse, not a bear. What do you want *me* to do about it?" and pulled the quilts back over his head.

To tell the truth I expected better of him, and told him so. Several times. Shaking his head, he finally emerged from the covers.

"Get the broom," he sighed, keeping *his* feet off the floor.

"*You* get it," I countered.

"We'll both get it," he said, struggling to his feet.

In the kitchen we located our weapons. Renaud took the mop; I took the broom. We tip-toed back to the bedroom to do battle, just as the mouse shot out from under the bed and ran wildly around the room with us in hot pursuit, waving mop and broom, until the mouse made a fast dash, right for Renaud's feet.

Braced against the three-and-a-half-foot-high footboard of the bed, mop held high for more momentum, Renaud yelled at the mouse, swung back with the mop, lost his balance and flew over the footboard, heels in the air. I dropped the broom, leaped onto the cedar chest, and the mouse streaked out of sight around the corner.

I looked down at Renaud, flat on the bed with knees draped over the footboard, feet dangling and mop still gripped tightly in his hands.

"Well," I said dryly, "we sure scared him."

But that was just a mouse. By the time I met the rat in the bathroom, which he had entered by enlarging Rosie Lecapable's pump drain hole, I was an old hand at dealing with wildlife, but a rat is a rat, and not to be considered lightly. I stifled a shriek of surprise, shut the door and went to the kitchen for an empty cardboard box and the dependable broom. I opened the bathroom door slowly, found my rat still waiting, dropped the carton over him and he was captured. It was easy. I was getting to be quite expert at the country life. But as soon as I let go of the box, it started moving, scooting across the floor. I directed it out into the hallway, held onto it so it wouldn't go anywhere and called Renaud.

"Renaud," I called softly. I didn't want to wake the children. They'd want to keep the rat as a pet.

"Renaud . . ."

Finally he responded.

"Uuuunnnnn?" he mumbled.

"Come here!"

"What?"

"Come here!"

"Why?"

"I've got a rat."

"A what?"

"Come here. Please!"

"Aww . . . noooo . . ."

"Renaud . . ."

"Huuummmmm?"

"Help!"

He came, but that just meant there were now two of us staring at the box. Finally we eased the box and our would-be tenant out of the hall, through the living room, out the front door and onto the lawn with its inch of soft, feathery snow. Shivering and chattering in the early morning chill, we hurried back to bed. In the morning, the box was still there at the end of a drunken trail in the snow, but the rat was gone. Probably back under the house again.

The gentlest of the rodents we encountered was aquamouse, whose sudden, splashing antics led us to the humidifier, where he was hanging for dear life onto the edge of the water reservoir with bony pink claws, hind parts of his body submerged and kicking up a storm. We rescued him, dried him off, showed him the door and sent him on his way.

Then there was the smart-alec rodent (a mouse or a rat —
we never found out which), who was smarter than we were
and stole bait from the traps under the sink and near the
pump without ever getting caught. The trap would spring
during the night and in the morning a clothespin, stick of
wood or dirty sock would be in the trap, the bait would be
gone and not a single rodent body could be found. I had the
feeling they were peeking around the corner at us, laughing.

* * * * ○ * * * *

CHAPTER 12

Watch Your Language

Although I couldn't speak a word of French when we got married, I was sure that within the year I would be speaking it like a native. I counted on it. But I counted wrong, because Renaud wasn't a good teacher and I wasn't a good student. Every victory over vocabulary, verbs, gender and sentence structure was won with sweat, jubilation and, quite often, embarrassment. This was in the days before French immersion, but I'd been thrown in the deep end.

The thing that slowed me down most was that for long stretches of time the only human voices I heard were my own, Renaud's and the children's. Mine was no help, of course; neither was Renaud's, because we never had time to talk anymore. When he wanted to tell me something, he needed me to understand right away, so he said it in English. The children, when they started talking, spoke English because that's what they heard from me all day.

Once or twice a month we visited my parents in Montreal. It was wonderful talking to them. There was no hesitating over words, groping for meanings, or loud conversations about people I didn't know. When my parents talked about Uncle Lloyd or Great Aunt Gladys, or Aunt Kaye and Aunt Polly and Cousins Dot, Connie, Margie and Bev, I knew who they meant.

When we visited Renaud's family, it was like being thrust into a hen-house. It was loving and friendly, but everyone talked at the same time. Very loudly. And try as I might, I found it impossible to knit the recognizable bits of vocabulary and mountains of unfamiliar names into meaning.

It might have been easier to learn French had my exposure to it been more gradual and frequent. But for days I'd be alone, then suddenly we'd be at a party, or a funeral, or in the midst of a Caza gathering where great clusters and tangles of people spoke only French.

I needed to know French for many good reasons. I needed to feel at home in the community. I needed to shop. I wanted to be able to talk with my in-laws. And I needed to get through to the local talent that came to repair all the things that needed repairing — which appeared to be everything, all the time.

In spite of my good intentions, French, in my hands, became almost a dangerous weapon, and in the wake of my terrible mistakes, people would look at me with the same glazed apprehension one might accord a live hand-grenade while casting sympathetic glances in Renaud's direction.

My errors were frequent, and they were no respecters of subject matter. Often, when someone reacted to my brand of French with the vacant stare of shock, I started over and pronounced my errors even more firmly. However, people were polite and tried to ignore these glaring desecrations with good grace. If Renaud was present, he would look gently at me and wince or gaze balefully off into space. Good friends either corrected me solemnly, laughed uproariously or snickered and flushed quite red. Storekeepers blanched, tradesmen sighed and in-laws trembled.

At first, as the pall of shyness fell over my struggle for understanding, I was upset when I found out what I'd really been saying. But repetition leads to bravery in even the most horrendous activities and so the carnage continued.

I did my best. Unfortunately, I didn't learn my new language as effortlessly as Renaud's sister Camille learned English. Nor were my errors charming and cute — like the ones my friend Georgette makes when speaking English. Georgette used to say that the icy sidewalk was "slippy" instead of slippery and the stores were "crowdy" instead of crowded, and when someone won at the Chamber of Commerce Casino Night, according to Georgette they'd hit the "jack-spot."

Cute was also when my sister-in-law said she was going to the chicken to put a kitchen in the oven. So were the errors made by my in-laws Romé and Bella when they traveled with us to Florida. One day, while watching the celebrity panel on a TV program, Romé said musingly, "I've heard of him before. Who's that fellow Macaroni anyway?"

"No, Pa," said Renaud. "It's Mickey Rooney."

"That's what I said — Macaroni."

And when the weather report followed the news one evening: "Where' that — Pepsi Cola?"

"No, Pa. It's Pensacola."

On a cooking show we watched with Bella one afternoon, when there was a dissertation on the use of garlic. Romé's eyes lit up with recognition. "I know what that is," he exclaimed. "There was a fellow who used to come around home looking for work a few years back, and he could speak the garlic."

"That's Gaelic, Pa," said Renaud.

But the one that topped them all came from Bella when we were sitting around in the evening in our motel room. Renaud read the newspaper, Romé worked on a French crossword puzzle brought from home, Bella knitted and I wrote postcards. The television droned away in the background with no one really paying attention, until a commercial came on for H & R Block, suggesting that they be allowed to take the worry out of your income tax returns.

"Hah! Listen to that," Renaud drawled, looking up from his newspaper. "They're even making commercials about income tax."

Eyes brightening at a familiar word, Bella looked up with interest from her knitting. "Huh, that's nothing new," she exclaimed. "Why, back home they've been advertising Kotex for years."

My errors, unlike these, were not usually cute. The French language itself seemed to have a lot of built-in booby-traps that made my errors insulting and sometimes downright dangerous. Many of my errors, in fact, could not be put down on paper, but others were little more than mildly offensive.

For example, the word for stove is *poêle*, dangerously close, in sound, to *poil*, a term for body hair. Imagine the startled expressions that greeted me when I innocently remarked, "My mother-in-law has avocado green body hair." Or the distressing observation that my own body hair had a self-cleaning oven. The possibilities were endless.

Take, for example, the time I woke up during the night, glanced out the window, saw a cottage on the point to the north of us engulfed in flames, called the local grocer, who was chief of the volunteer fire department, and insisted loud and clear that there was a big "*fou*" (fool) not "*feu*" (fire) on the point and would they come to put it out.

It didn't help either that everyone talked so fast and changed subjects in mid-sentence, so that I was still sorting verbs about the trip back to the sugar bush, while trying to catch a few words about the new hours for mass and a few others about the weekly specials at the local supermarket. No wonder my head was spinning. I remained undaunted, however, and plowed ahead, most often answering questions with a three-subject delay. And in face-to-face conversation, my answers were a combination of lightning-quick piecing together and pure guesswork — a dangerous undertaking, considering that my comprehension was like those conversations overheard in a bus: "Are you and Renaud _____ to the _____ tomorrow _____ _____ _____ because _____ and the _____ certainly _____ ." It was hard work and awfully tiring on the brain.

People were understanding, though, when I said such things as "Renaud and I were chasing a *sourire* (smile) around the house," when we were really after a *souris* (mouse).

Another complication of language was numbers, which you might think would be fairly straightforward. After all, one is "*un,*" two is "*deux,*" three is "*trois,*" etc. But let me tell you, though I might still be in there pitching even after ten, I'm not even in the same ballpark when we get up there where seventy-eight is *soixante-dix-huit* (sixty-ten-eight) and ninety-eight is *quatre-vingt-dix-huit* (four-twenties, ten-eight). Try playing Bingo to that! Or, for that matter, singing "Ninety-nine bottles of beer on the wall."

Then there's the matter of gender and the fact that in French everything from books, cars, beans, fire engines, animals and bugs to individual body parts are given a sexual identity.

"What do you call a fly?" I asked Renaud. "It might be male or female, but you just call it *la mouche*. What if it happens that it's a male fly, would you call it *le la mouche*?"

I was looking for clarification, but all Renaud would say was, "If you really have to know that, you must have darn good eyesight."

CHAPTER 13

* * * * O * * * *

Born to Argue: The Great Blueberry Explosion and the Time the Shotgun Went Off in the Outhouse

One of the best exercises in learning French was exposure to family stories, which were delivered a mile a minute and interspersed with gestures, laughter and interruptions for corrections or additional detail.

After a while I caught on to key words and knew what story was being told. Then I followed along, piecing the words I recognized together with what I knew the story to be.

Everyone loved to hear the stories repeated, and every storyteller added his own embellishments and special manner of delivery. Eventually I came to enjoy the stories as much as anybody and began to think of tales about Jean-Baptiste Le-Beau-dit-Caza and all the other storied family characters as though they were mine.

There was the uncle who told everyone at the supper table that the salty soup was far too fresh, urging them to pour lots of salt into it before they tasted it, personally helping them toward that end, against strong protest, by hurrying around the table with the salt shaker, then sitting back to enjoy the predictable results.

And the other uncle who had, by reason of seniority, first crack at the bowl of favorite hot, buttered macaroni, and one mealtime, dumped the entire contents onto his own plate. The big-eyed Caza children stared disbelievingly, but dared not raise a voice in protest.

My favorite family character, though, was Uncle Zenon. Everybody had stories about Uncle Zenon, a well-traveled, well-read gentleman with a strong tendency to argue. He never married, although one time he came close. After courting his sweetheart, Fortunata, for several years, one evening he slicked himself up and went to propose marriage. But he got cold feet at the last minute, kept going, hopped a train west and didn't return for two years.

Uncle Zenon was a cheerful, stocky man with a pronounced limp and, in later years, a noticeable tremor. He kept bees and produced the best honey in the countryside. Children passing his home on their way from school loved to stop by because it was well known that Uncle Zenon kept a wooden spoon and a jar of honey at the ready. As they approached him, he took the sticky spoon out of his waistcoat pocket and shook a bit of honey into it for each in turn. With the honey, plus the tremor, a lot of children arrived home sticky.

When Uncle Zenon returned from his early travels, he was filled with knowledge of world events and science and was eager to convey his findings to the villagers. But his words fell on deaf ears, because nobody believed his stories of faraway places, the developing world and feats of engineering marvel. The majority rules, and when gathered around the old pot-bellied stove in Quenneville's village store, Uncle Zenon's friends would vote him down and declare him wrong if he ventured some obscure fact about, let's say, Jupiter's moons. That was all right with Uncle Zenon, who was noted for lighting conversational fuses for the sheer joy of argument.

This trait cut through succeeding generations and was cultivated and enlarged upon to a fine and sometimes pointless degree by nearly every Caza — male and female. It was the favorite pastime of Renaud and his father.

But nobody explained that to me.

For years I listened helplessly to the loud, gestured, sounds-like-fighting-to-me exchanges that went on. I listened to Renaud and his father arguing about such things as the height of a telephone pole, the thickness of the ice, at what time the leaves started falling from the maple tree out front last year, whether a sauce was good or bad, whether it tasted like the sauce Grandma used to make, why it was better or worse and why it will never again taste as good as it used to.

The irrelevancy of their arguments made me want to get involved, too. I wanted to settle disputes and tell them, "Cut that out!" Two things held me back: the language barrier and not being a Caza.

Finally I had my chance to participate. Every January when we traveled to Florida with Renaud's parents, Renaud and his father argued about the length of the motel room. It was twenty-one feet long, Renaud said. No, his father insisted, it was twenty-two feet long.

"No, twenty-one!"

"Twenty-two!"

They paced up and down, measuring each step carefully, and never agreeing. This went on every year, at every motel.

One winter I brought a tape measure along on our holiday so we could settle the argument once and for all. That's when I realized that the size of the room was of no consequence. They weren't arguing to prove a point, but simply for the joy of their own brand of social discourse. They loved to argue. The tape measure stayed hidden in my suitcase.

I thought the Cazas were a lucky family. I didn't understand them, but I liked and admired them. I admired especially Renaud's mother, who raised her large family under circumstances that would have left us more liberated women flinching. If I thought the early days of our marriage were primitive, I was certainly not the pioneer my mother-in-law was.

Bella had a big house and eight young Cazas to raise. In the early days of her household, long before I joined the family, instead of refrigerator-freezers, electric ranges and vacuum cleaners, there were ice boxes, wood stoves and many willing and unwilling hands.

Renaud's family raised, besides commercial crops of tobacco and hops, most of their own food, including meat. I was in awe of anyone who could convert a large animal into steaks, roasts, stew meat and hamburger, stuff her own sausages and turn chickens into (besides eggs and chicken fricassee) everything from feather mattresses and pillows, to clothing from the calico-print fabric of the feed bags.

It was no picnic to be a housewife on the farm in those days. The men plowed the fields, brought in the grain and put corn in the silo. That left the womenfolk to do the lighter stuff, like milking, scrubbing pails and separators, planting, weeding and harvesting the kitchen garden, canning meats, fruits and vegetables for winter, feeding field hands, bearing children, knitting, sewing, mending and transforming scraps of leftover cotton into magnificent quilts.

A farm is a business with all the problems of an urban business and the added advantage or disadvantage of most of the employees being family. As they got older, they enjoyed telling about the homey incidents they had lived through in the crowded, exciting past. Like the jar of "worked" blueberries that Renaud's sister Andrée brought up from the cellar for a Sunday supper dessert.

"I was ten years old," said Andrée, "and we were all sitting at the kitchen table eating supper. Then Ma said, 'Andrée, you go down to the cellar and bring up a jar of blueberries for dessert.'

"As I started down the cellar stairs, she called after me, 'Andrée, be careful with them. Don't bound up the steps.'

"Well," said Andrée, "I didn't like the cellar. None of us did. It was dark and damp and spidery there. So I was in a hurry to get out. Picking up the first jar I came to, I ran up the stairs. Then I raced across the kitchen and handed the jar of blueberries to Ma.

"That's when we heard it. A loud hissing sound. Ma and I both had our hands on the jar, and we froze. Everybody in the room froze. I shouldn't have been running up the stairs with a possibly fermented jar of fruit.

"Ma said, 'You ran with it!' I said, 'I forgot,' Ma said, 'It's going to explode!'

"Every eye in the room was fixed hypnotically on us, holding that jar of blueberries. Suddenly, the top flew off with a *sssssizzzING*. All eyes swiveled upward to follow the purple geyser of blueberries as they erupted out of the jar and swooshed up to hit the ceiling.

"They were those small, wild blueberries, picked by all us kids in the August heat of the Teafields. There must have been a million blueberries in that jar. At least, that's what it seemed like.

"There were blueberries hanging from the ceiling, clinging to the curtains, windows, tablecloth and unprotected heads, and oozing down the walls.

"Our kitchen was old-fashioned. The ceiling was the kind made of two-inch strips of wood, grooved and put together with cracks where the strips join. Well, hundreds of blueberries slid into those cracks and stuck there in rows, like gleaming blue beads on a string. And some of them hung loose, festooned in dripping garlands of blue syrup.

"Pa, he was standing off to one side and didn't get a drop on him. He shook his head, as if to say, 'Certainly none of this is *my* doing!'

"Ma just sighed like business-as-usual. She threw a dish-towel over her head and walked back and forth under the cracks, using a dinner knife to flick blueberries from their crevasses along the ceiling, while all of us berry-blue kids headed for the pump and washbasin."

Then there was the time their mother prepared a big granite pot of beans for supper. As the hungry young family wedged themselves companionably around the table awaiting the savory beans, Mrs. Caza removed the heavy pot from the stove, held it in one hand with a pot holder, and gripped the ladle in the other hand. About to make a point in the conversation that was going on, she gestured widely, flinging both hands outward. The granite pot flipped over and the contents cascaded to the floor in a steaming, brown heap, bits of salt pork sliding casually down the side.

The kitchen was silent as necks craned upward and hungry eyes stared downward at their lost supper.

"My beans," exclaimed Mrs. Caza. "Oh, my beans, my beans!"

"That's the way it is around here," growled Mr. Caza, shaking his head in resignation. "Why do these things always have to happen to this family?"

Of course, Mr. Caza was really no stranger to the consequences of large-family life, since he was one of nine children himself. I'm sure he will always remember clearly the time the gun went off in the out-house. That was when two of his sisters, aged eight and ten, discovered that if they excused themselves from the supper table early and went to sit in the two-seater privy, they could escape dish-washing chores at the pump in the kitchen.

Seated in their dim shelter every night after supper, they entertained themselves by chatting, giggling and browsing through the Eaton's catalogue. But it was not long before Euclide and Romé caught on to their sisters' after-supper duplicity and began to plot revenge. One day they hit upon a plan.

Advancing stealthily to the back of the privy, they pointed the barrel of a shotgun through a knot-hole, pulled the trigger and sent it blasting into the fulsome heaps under the privy seats.

The roar of the blast, plus the fallout, resulted in the hurried departure of two uninjured but frightened and smelly little girls who were too preoccupied as they ran straight to the house to notice two jubilant brothers fleeing like rabbits in the opposite direction.

Of course, the stories I liked best were the ones that involved Renaud. There was the time he and his brother Maurice, ages nine and eleven, were sent to gather eggs. Struck with inspiration when a freshly curled, bossy and neat-as-a-pin sister ordered them to get eggs for Mother's baking "right this minute," the boys, who had a treasure trove of vintage eggs stashed away, placed them delicately into the basket and crossed the yard to where their sister stood waiting. As she approached to take the basket, the boys ran forward, yelling in unison, "Here they are!" They swung back, then forward, and let her have it — right on the head. Rotten eggs flowed over her shiny curls, down her face and neck and over her nice clean dress as the boys quickly shifted into reverse and streaked out of sight behind the barn. Who could resist such a family?

✳ ✳ ✳ ✳ ○ ✳ ✳ ✳ ✳

CHAPTER 14

Party Poopers Anonymous

The social life I led as a single woman bore no resemblance to the world in which Renaud expected me to function.

Single, my social life was simple. After work I either stayed home or went out. If I stayed home, I read, worked on my stamp collection, painted or wrote letters. If I went out, it was either with girl friends or with a current boy friend. If it was girl friends, we went to a movie, took walks or went to house parties. If it was a date with a boy friend, we went to a movie, a bar and grill or a restaurant. All this easy-going socializing didn't prepare me for country social life as a woman married to a hometown boy.

As soon as the honeymoon was over, I was launched into Renaud's social orbit to spectate or participate in everything he pursued. I watched him goal at hockey, bat at baseball and followed him around the country fairs, tractor pulls and boxing matches and stock-car races he enjoyed. I even joined a bowling league with him for seven years, during which time I won the high handicap award three years in a row before they discontinued it to avoid further embarrassment to me.

There was ice fishing (all night) at Ste.-Anne-de-la-Pérade, a quaint village of fishing shacks set up on the river ice, where hundreds of people gather to fish for tommy-cod.

There were cleared walkways, even streetlights in rows among the gaily painted shacks that ranged in size from the dimensions of a small closet to those of a walk-in closet. Each shack had a little stove with a black chimney sticking through the roof and each also had a hole in the plywood floor and through the ice, around which lumpy, winter-garbed tenants sat on boxes or blocks of wood, hunched over, dropping baited hooks into the dark water, and waiting.

It was charming, but scarcely comfortable. It didn't take long to realize that Renaud, myself and three friends would emerge pretty cramped and weary from a night of being squeezed tighter than any self-respecting sardine, or tommy-cod — even though we took turns sleeping on the woodpile.

Of course, I expected some friction within the framework of our social life — partly because of our backgrounds being so different, along with the fact that I had been brought up in a dry province. There was also the realization that any marriage anywhere means that two people with different tastes, friends, social leanings and priorities are welded to-gether and someone has to bend.

It didn't take long to find out who would do the leaning and who would do the bending.

It had nothing to do with trying to change a man who was set in his ways, because I didn't. But he changed anyway. Perhaps not from being the person he was, but certainly from being the person I had been dating for two years.

Before marriage, for instance, when we visited nightclubs or our favorite bar and grill for the evening, Renaud went all out to please me. Attentive and gallant, he held doors open for me, danced with me, hovered over me solicitously, pro-tected me from bumbling drunks, stuck to me like Velcro tape and, after two and a half hours of partying, he asked in a concerned voice, full of tenderness, if I was tired (he really did!)

Even the heart-deep sorrow of parting bore its own magic, and when we snuggled together in the car for a goodnight kiss and he gazed into my eyes and called me *"mon trésor,"* I longed for the time when such charming romantics could go on and on . . . forever.

Basking in the glow of importance generated by Renaud's devotion, I wished that I could stay out as late as I pleased, instead of having to be home when Mom and Dad said. But we have to be careful what we wish for in this life, because we just might get it.

And it didn't take long. After I was signed, sealed and delivered, so to speak, I discovered the demands of married social life, the ferocious loyalty of the gathering of the Clan Caza, the significance of family parties and the fact that sleep is important.

What's more, Renaud no longer catered to me by asking where and when we might party and un-party, and I discovered that wives are not in the same league as girl friends.

Wives, it seems, don't have to be home at a sensible hour. Wives, accompanied by husbands, can stay out until dawn (whether they want to or not). They can even end up at a friend's, neighbor's, in-law's or total stranger's house for breakfast. Or vice versa. And the party rolls on. And on.

With a girl friend, a man has to hang onto his dignity and decorum. He has to be attentive and reasonable. With a wife, however, he is entitled to get good and looped.

As a girl friend, all that was expected of me was to be there, secure in the peaceful ambiance created by my solicitous fiancé. As a wife, however, I was often expected to sit alone at the table while he ambled off to have a few thousand words with someone across the dance hall — more often than not somebody he had been with all day at work.

I was also expected to be a good sport and polka with the old pal with pasted-down hair and beady eyes, who bore a startling resemblance to a Fort Lauderdale seagull, and do-se-do with that blank-looking fellow wearing his belt up under his armpits, who smells, for some inexplicable reason, exactly like an old, dusty velour train seat. Now I like dancing as much as anyone, but a certain mood is an advantage, and this wasn't it.

Because of the friendly nature of the local watering hole, the traffic was nearly always shoulder to jawbone, the local band or disco made up in volume what it lacked in mood, and too often the only possible conversation was: "Do you wanna 'nother drink?"

My introduction to married social life took place soon after the honeymoon when someone Renaud and the whole village knew was giving a party. As soon as we arrived, Renaud introduced me to a couple of old regulars named "Thirteen Cents" and "Pay you Friday." Then he squeezed us in at a table with six other couples I didn't know, which couldn't be helped, because I didn't know anybody, and left me there while he circulated to say "hello" to half the village.

I can take one drink comfortably, then nurse a second and perhaps a third along for the next seven hours or so, but by evening's end, there were usually several full glasses in front of me. Everyone was friendly and eager that I should have a good time, another drink and "Aw, c'mon — be a good shport!" Why these statements were considered synonomous was never clear. After all, while it could perhaps have been considered "shporty" of me to drink all the gin in the bar, I have never considered being violently ill as having a good time.

My idea of a good time is to go to almost anything live — a play, concert or recital — or to go out with, or stay home with, friends, and meet other friends (or strangers) who are interesting, fairly well informed and/or talented and who like to talk. Not gossip — talk.

My idea of a good party is a plain but tasty buffet or sit-down dinner (preferably Chinese), preceded by a cocktail or two, followed perhaps by dancing and just enough drinks to settle a mellow glow on the company.

There should, ideally, be barely discernible background music, heard clearly only on the dance floor and, since I hardly ever have a good time confined anywhere for more than eight hours, in my dream world the party would disband somewhere in the area of midnight to 2:00 A.M. with everyone being conscious enough to drive home safely.

Renaud's idea of a good party is a twelve-hour stint with good buddies at the local bar.

There's nothing friendlier than the social life of a country village. We live in an area where the mere dropping of a hat is an excuse to throw a whing-ding. There are mixers, wedding receptions, political dinners, benefits for this and that, card parties, bingo, fund raisings for sports activities, bowling dances, hockey dances, golf tournament dances, Chamber of Commerce casino night, the Optimists, "thank you parties" and even, so help me, "you're welcome parties" (a rare phenomenon that came into being when two duck hunters capsized their boat in the channel. Heavy in their soaked autumn gear, the hunters were unable to swim for shore or right their overturned boat and climb back. After they were rescued, they threw a great "thank you" party, which was followed a month or so later by the rescuers sponsoring a "you're welcome" party).

Then there are bean suppers, fish suppers, spaghetti suppers, corn boil parties, oyster parties, pancake breakfasts, brunches and summer barbecues. To say nothing of the springtime sugar bush parties with trestle tables set up in log cabins in the woods, where we're served grillade, potatoes, home-baked beans, crusty bread, eggs, bacon, ham and pancakes loaded with maple syrup.

So don't waste any sympathy on these poor country folk living out their dull lives far from the glittering yippee of the big city. Believe me, there's plenty of yippee out here in hay country.

In the first couple of decades of our marriage there were Saturday night dances in one place or another close to home almost on a weekly basis. The orchestra is bound to strike up a Paul Jones, then a square dance gets underway. A couple of old-timers do a step dance to deafening applause and cheers. Then there's a flurry of folk songs, and a fiddler demonstrates a toe-tapping, knee-slapping jig. And so the evening goes along: charming, colorful, kindly and even fun. But by five in the morning, I've had enough.

After the first ten years of this happy partying, I thought it was time for things to mellow a bit. But the St. Anicet social life roared along its predetermined path, bowling over on-lookers, bystanders and outsider spouses. After a while, I complained heatly to Renaud. It didn't do any good, though, and my poor sportsmanship made the air tense around the Caza compound for days afterwards.

The last full-fledged party we went to before I put my foot down and said I would go to parties but would leave when the sensible people did, was a summer perch supper and beer bash. By 2:00 A.M. the sensible people and even the orchestra had gone. The earlier roar of a couple of hundred people all talking at once became a muted blur of lifelong friendship declarations emanating from a few fellows draped around the bar.

"Let's go home," I said.

Renaud said he was having fun and wanted to stay. Time marched on.

Much later, Renaud said, in response to my reproachful look, "We're just starting to have a good time."

"But it's five o'clock in the morning," I protested.

"That's not late," he argued. "Look, there's still some people here." He gestured widely. Indeed there were. Five men in shirtsleeves were leaning on a table in the far left-hand corner, drinking with grim intensity. To the right were two couples, holding hands and looking dead. On the dance floor one glued-together couple shuffled sluggishly to no music.

"Well, why do we have to stay just because there's someone else here?" I complained.

"These are my friends," said Renaud, genuinely hurt by my attitude. It meant nothing to him that 95 percent of the original revelers at this party shared my sentiments that the evening was finished and were now sound asleep in their own beds.

"I know they're your friends," I agreed. "But most of the people are gone."

"Aw, come on, we're having such a good time."

This was news to me.

By eight o'clock in the morning, Renaud, though disappointed, admitted that we may as well go home, since everyone else had already done so. Even the ones that had to be peeled off the bar and carried out. Except that Albert, the hotel keeper, was still there (waiting to lock up so he could go to bed, for heaven's sake), but Renaud seemed to be waiting for *him* to go home first and didn't want to hurt his feelings by leaving.

Eventually Albert, chatting casually, edged us doorward. We crossed the threshold, the door clicked shut softly and we headed for the car. Renaud was smiling, relaxed and happy and I, with such seething seas and currents raging within me, could scarcely keep from banging my head on the pavement of the parking lot.

* * * * ○ * * * *

CHAPTER 15

Boys Will Be Boys

My good humor got stretched to the limit by the partying stamina of those around me. But it wasn't just the partying that tried my patience. There were things like hunting in the woods up north, when six of the fellows decided to let a couple of us wives come along.

It was November. I was seven months pregnant and proud that Renaud wanted me along on this manly expedition. I felt cherished and needed, so I went.

We drove there in two cars, parked at the edge of a forest path, unloaded our provisions and hiked a mile through crunchy leaves, covered with a thin crust of snow, to the cabin.

There were two large rooms in the cabin — the kitchen and the bunk room. There was no electricity and no plumbing.

The other wife and I soon realized that we were not brought along to trek companionably through the woods with our macho husbands or even for the pure pleasure of our delightful, feminine presence. We were brought along to take care of cabin K.P. and accommodate six big meat-and-potato appetites. And it was obvious that the men figured they were doing us a favor.

The first evening, smoke hung in the after-supper air as

the men settled into hunting stories, remembering last year when Benny packed the sandwiches and ate his early because he said he hadn't had much breakfast. At noon, when the rest of them were famished, they sat around and opened their lunch packs to find he'd given each six slices of dry bread. No butter, no filling.

"Chris' — were you guys ever sore — Ha, ha, he, he, ho . . ."

After we women cleared the table, washed and put away the dishes and swept the floor, all eight of us retired en masse to the bunk room. I took the lower of one bunk bed and Renaud took the upper.

After a while, the fire in the little stove went out. There weren't enough blankets, and no warm husband to snuggle up to. As I shivered violently and peered between the long cracks in the log wall at the snow on the ground outside, I just knew I wouldn't be able to make it through the night without at least one visit to the privy, which was a hundred feet from the cabin door in the dark, snowy bush.

My emotions were mixed, they weren't easy to sort out. I was happy to be invited. Happy to be away on a week-end with Renaud. But I was also pregnant, dying to use the facilities, and very cold.

Renaud, on the other hand, was entirely happy. Happy to be hunting with the guys, happy I was with him, happy that I was pregnant, happy, happy, happy.

I didn't have to look far to see who was doing the better job of adjusting to the merging of these two solitudes.

It's a good thing I liked Renaud's family. It helped me get through situations that called for special reserves of patience. Like the boys-will-be-boys syndrome. Occasionally the cast of characters changed, but Renaud, brother-in-law Maurice and cousin Raymond were the most trying. My first experience was when the three of them went out for a beer a few miles away, across the U.S. border, and stayed there thirty-six hours.

Finally cousin Raymond rested his head on the table and couldn't be roused. Full of cousinly concern, and with tears in their eyes for the apparently dear departed, Renaud and Maurice called a doctor, who was also county coroner, and who hurried right over in his pyjamas and raincoat.

It was 4:00 A.M. when the good doctor arrived, examined the "corpse" draped over the table, glared at Renaud and Maurice, snorted and strode indignantly out of the bar and back home to bed. The corpse recovered, slightly the worse for wear, after a good night's sleep.

After that, I was never the same and cousin Raymond approached me with caution when looking for Renaud. He had reason to be wary. The time he and Renaud appeared at the back door as the sun edged up over the horizon one Sunday morning, after an all-night session of camaraderie, I had paced the floor for part of the night and dozed fitfully on and off as morning approached. I was in no mood to be talked into a good humor by these two happy men at daybreak.

They told me what a wonderful person I was. They told me I wasn't mad at them. That I was Renaud's understanding wife and Raymond's good friend. Then they demanded breakfast.

I went into the bathroom, yanked two bathing suits off the doorknob, returned, handed them to the men and gritted out from between my clenched, friendly, smiling teeth, "Go — jump — in — the — lake!"

They paused and looked at me in surprise. Renaud seemed to think that I didn't get the picture. "No, Margie dear," he said, giving me a weak smile. "Be nice," he said. "Make us a good cup of coffee and some breakfast."

"Get into those bathing suits and into the lake this minute," I hissed.

"Look," protested Renaud. "Don't get mad. We haven't done anything wrong. Honest."

"Yes," agreed Raymond. "We're perfec'ly shober," he said, hiccupping gently and leaning on Renaud, who was supporting himself on the kitchen sink.

"Do you want to go in for a swim with your clothes on, or do you want to change first" I remarked coldly.

Moaning and complaining bitterly, they surprised me by believing my threat, took the bathing suits, went into the bedroom and changed.

They shivered as they trailed out the door, across the lawn and into the lake. The lake was cold. It did my heart good.

I don't think I was unreasonable, but to this day, to hear cousin Raymond tell it, I picked up the two men bodily, fully clothed and flung them off the pier. Of course, I wouldn't want to disillusion him. I want to keep that fear right there where it'll do the most good.

It was only after I saw for myself that Renaud and Raymond were up to their waists in the lake that I came back in to start breakfast.

By now the children were awake and rocketing around the house with the dog — energetic, happy and noisy, as befits anyone young who's had a decent night's sleep.

When the men came back from their reluctant swim, dripping and shivering in the doorway and hoping for a little warmth and a kind word, I sent them to change and put their breakfasts on the table.

After breakfast, Renaud went to bed and Raymond walked unsteadily outside to collapse in a lawn chair on the shore, facing the healing lake breeze.

After a while I took a cup of fresh coffee out to him. He looked up with eyes full of gratitude for this little sign of truce. "I'll just sit here for a while," he said in a whisper, gripping the steaming cup with both hands.

I nodded, picked up a quilt from the clothesline and draped it over his trembling knees. "See that big boat over there?" he said, pointing to the southwest end of the St. Lawrence Seaway. I looked across the lake, then back at him. He was perfectly serious.

"I'll just sit here until that boat gets out of sight, beyond the point, then I'll get up and go home," he said meekly.

I looked at him again, then back at the big boat. "Uuh-Hummm . . ." I said, then returned to the house. The children and I watched on and off from the kitchen window as cousin Raymond shakily drank his coffee and patiently waited for the solidly imbedded Furey Island, with the Johnson lighthouse on it, to move out of sight around the point.

Boys will be boys.

* * * * * ○ * * * *

CHAPTER 16

And What Would You *Wear to a Bouillotte?*

When I was twenty and single, what to wear wasn't a problem. I went to work, lounged around the house, went out. I wore suits and office dresses to work; whatever I wanted around the house. Evenings out were dressy.

Then Renaud and I got married and suddenly everything changed. I was in a different milieu, and my what-to-wear signals were no longer on automatic. I didn't need a fashion coordinator. What I needed was an interpreter, an ear to the what-everyone-else-is-wearing grapevine and a little in-house cooperation.

As it was, I had access to none of these things, and from the beginning I was awash with doubts and made bad decisions.

For one thing, there was a new sort of partying going on. There were traditional French Canadian things I'd never heard of. Suddenly I, who had once adored parties, began to dread them — not only for their unfamiliarity and longevity, but because fashion-wise I was always in the soup.

I not only didn't know what to expect of most of the local functions, but my waistline expanded, my budget shrank and my world became more and more restricted to childhood diseases, family pets, keeping water in the pipes and food on the table. It was easy to lose sight of what was going on in the world beyond our walls. So when we had to go to big dinners, conventions or construction shows, I ended up looking hopefully into my closet, saying "eenie, meenie, miney, mo" and, appropriate or not, I had my outfit for the occasion.

Most of the time I was torn between being glad to get out of the house and being paranoid about my appearance. I nearly always felt as though I was trailing limply in the wake of Renaud's white-hot enthusiasm like a piece of toilet tissue stuck to the bottom of a shoe.

Renaud, used to the local social scene, also happens to be one of those infuriating people who has little interest in clothes but always looks great in whatever he wears. Because of his own confidence, no matter how much an outsider I was, Renaud took it for granted that I knew what I was doing, and turned out to be totally useless as a sounding board. He didn't understand what it was I didn't understand, and watched curiously as I readied myself for one social function after the other, not offering so much as a raised eyebrow to tip me off that I was about to make a damn fool of myself.

The first time Renaud bought tickets to a *bouillotte* at the hotel in the village I asked, "A *bouillotte*? What's that?"

"Oh, it's a party," he said, "with supper, then dancing."

"What should I wear?" I asked.

Renaud shrugged and said "Anything."

Renaud doesn't have an extensive wardrobe, and I admire his approach to the matter of clothing, which is that he can only wear one thing at a time. All he needs is some work clothes, a good suit, a jacket and a few shirts and slacks. I, with a low-budget but more extensive wardrobe, never have quite the right thing. Maybe he's right. I worry too much.

Renaud always makes sense. But I still can't reconcile myself
to the idea that women can get away with wearing the same
thing to a reception at the Queen Elizabeth Hotel, a Carib-
bean cruise, a class reunion at the university and a bean
supper at the Parish Hall.

I would have to figure out the *bouillotte* for myself. Party,
supper and dance. Ah, a supper dance. So I brought out my
sheer, lettuce-leaf-green chiffon with draped neckline and
sheath skirt and a dainty crystal-and-amber necklace, and
didn't even notice, what with the rush of dressing, feeding
the baby, picking up Gisèle, our babysitter, and gathering
compact and lipstick together, that Renaud was smiling
gently and being very quiet.

We drove to the hotel for the *bouillotte*, and as soon as we
stepped through the doorway I realized I was overdressed.
The room was hot and smoky, there was a deafening roar of
loud laughing voices, bottles and glasses clashed, music,
laughter and shouting competed. But what caught my attention was all the slacks, jeans, T-shirts, shorts and sandals.

This wasn't at all what I expected. A *bouillotte*, it was now
clear, was a sporty, indoor beach party free-for-all, featuring
a mammoth stew, cooked in tubs and served catch-as-catch-
can, along with large chunks of crusty bread, on aluminum
pie plates with plastic forks.

"Why didn't you tell me?" I wailed to Renaud as soon as
I got him cornered.

"I thought you knew," he said calmly.

"If I knew everyone was going to be dressed like *this* would
I have dressed like *this*?" I asked furiously.

"Well, you might," he said. "I thought you knew but
wanted to look like a big-shot." Which comment, considering
that I now looked like a big-stupid, made me want to push
his head in his beer.

It wasn't the first time I wished Renaud wouldn't always

assume I knew what I was doing. And it certainly wasn't the last.

There was the big party in Montreal, where everyone wore long gowns and looked perfectly elegant, and I wore a nice but very out-of-place tailored suit. And the party at the Holiday Inn, where I wore a long gown and everyone else wore pant suits. How do they *know*?

There was also the oyster party. I'd never been to one before. I'm allergic to oysters and don't like beer, but I reasoned that surely there would be other things on the menu. The party was a reception at a heavy equipment dealership in a Montreal showroom. I wore a cocktail dress, high-heeled sandals and a nervous twitch when I discovered that trestle tables were set up all over the concrete floor of the display area. There were no chairs. Everyone else was wearing sweaters and slacks, and I didn't know a soul except Renaud, who gestured expansively and said, "Here — have some oysters," then disappeared. It lasted seven hours!

By now I was used to getting things wrong, so on the drive home it would have been pointless to tell Renaud how miserable I'd been, because he would have smiled cheerfully and said that there must be something wrong with me because he had a perfectly wonderful time.

CHAPTER 17

* * * * ○ * * * *

The Joyous Holiday Season or I Know What I Want to Deck, and It Isn't the Halls

Probably the greatest learning experience of my new life took place shortly after our November marriage. It was December, and a married Christmas.

I come from a small family — Mom and Dad, my brother and me. There were Christmas stockings, a candlelight church service, gifts under the tree and Christmas dinner. And with that, the holiday season was over. New Year's, a week later, aside from a few whisps of "Auld Lang Syne," was nothing.

I expected no more, no less in my new station as the bride of a French Canadian man.

Six weeks after we were married, we celebrated Christmas by going to Midnight Mass in St. Anicet. It was charming. After Mass, we were engulfed in a blizzard of *Joyeux Noël* greetings outside the church, where Renaud introduced me to dozens of local people with names I'd never heard of. Names like: Castagnier, Faubert, Dumouchel, Deschambault, Lefebvre and Quenneville.

That was just the beginning. Renaud, who is the dearest, most sensitive person in the world in most respects, is infuriating in his belief in the school of thought that maintains a non-swimmer should be thrown bodily, and unprepared, into very deep water and will then, of necessity, learn to swim. Thus was I plunged into the local Holiday Season.

"Let's go to Ma's after Mass", Renaud said.

"All right," I agreed, clinging happily to his arm as we scurried through the milling crowd and drifting snow toward the car.

"We won't stay long," said Renaud, "but it's a tradition in French Canadian families for the children to gather at their parents' homes after Midnight Mass for coffee and a little lunch. It's called *Réveillon*."

Renaud's idea of a little drop-in-midnight-lunch turned out to be more along the lines my family might expect of a church picnic for an entire congregation.

After threading our way around the parked cars in the driveway, stamping snow off our boots in the woodshed leading to the back door, we went into the kitchen, where we were promptly mobbed by a tidal wave of the loudest, merriest bunch of people I'd ever seen, packed into the stove area near the kitchen door. It was a delightful, if somewhat overwhelming, sight, with welcoming arms hugging and everybody talking and laughing at once.

Savory steam wafted up from the stove, with its pots of *ragout boulette* (meatball stew), chicken legs and spicy *tourtières* (pork pies). A long table in the center of the room was crowded with baskets of crusty bread, bowls of salads, dishes of olives, pickles and relishes. The buffet was aglow with candles flanking a chocolate yule log and mounds of cookies, squares, cakes and macaroons.

I was suctioned along with the flow of the crowd that surged from kitchen to living room, and on the way caught glimpses of babies sleeping in the tumble of coats in the master bedroom off the kitchen. The whole house seethed with spicy smells and noise as everyone moved about, talked, laughed and crowded into the big country living room where the Christmas tree stood waiting for the family gift-giving that would take place at New Year's. This worked well as a compromise for us, because it meant that Christmas could be spent with my parents, and New Year's with Renaud's family.

On that first Christmas, my French was nearly nonexistent, and Renaud was the only one in his family who spoke English. Because he was also the only one there I really knew (I sometimes wondered about that), I clung to him with the tenacity of fly to flypaper — though with his sink-or-swim attitude, he was far too busy being a totally involved member of the family to translate the impossible volume of conversation that rose to a raucous crescendo whenever the Clan Caza assembled.

That first Christmas Eve encounter of en-masse Cazas was followed Christmas Day by a quiet gathering at my parent's home. Then New Year's Eve came, and Renaud and I, along with some of his brothers and sisters and their girl friends/boy friends, went for a spirited night on the town at a low-ceilinged bar and grill across the border in northern New York State, where I was introduced to a mild and inoffensive drink called *crème de cocoa* (it was a lot more offensive by the next morning). We rang in the New Year until 6:00 A.M. and were home and in bed around eight, with the big New Year's Day family reunion a scant few hours away.

When we got to Renaud's parents' home shortly after noon, the place was already buzzing. Everyone greeted everyone with *Bonne et Heureuse Année* greetings, then Renaud hurried me along into the living room, threw himself into a soft chair and pretended to be settled in for the day. In reality he was merely coiling for an abrupt sprint out the door at the first opportunity. Opportunity showed up in the form of his brothers Yves and Avila. Renaud leaped out of the chair, said that the men were going out to say hello to half the countryside (his exact words were "We're going to wish the neighbors a Happy New Year"), shot through the living room and into the kitchen, where he and his entourage put on boots and coats, and off they went. I was alone. Well, maybe not alone. But take my word for it, I might as well have been.

After a while, I noticed that couples who came into the house, after brief flurries of conversation and hug-and-kiss greetings, split apart like crevasses in an earthquake: the women and children took off their coats and boots, but the men, after a lot of loud discussion, left. To look for the ones who'd left earlier, they said.

It took several New Year's celebrations for me to realize that this whole routine was a highly polished device that allowed the men to get together and have a good time dropping in on old pals around the countryside. And instead of accepting all this with mild impatience as the other women did, I stewed and simmered and felt even more alone. In fact, I came to look forward with dread to the family's New Year's parties, because although my small-family Christmas was the comfortable, sober sort and Renaud's family Christmas was the religious time, there was nothing holy about a Caza New Year.

The men always came back sooner or later. Perhaps because they wanted to, but more likely because the people they visited were looking forward to their own private family parties and had edged them politely out the door.

I especially remember the New Year's that the men returned to the house to discover that brother Maurice had not surfaced. It was after seven, and the children, hungry and over-excited, were crowded around the tree and around the table; they spilled things and occasionally pushed someone smaller or hit someone bigger on the head with something hard, then ran to hide. The meal and gift-giving couldn't get under way with one member of the family missing, though, so a phone call was made to rouse Maurice, who said, "Sonofabitch, you woke me up," and "Chris' . . . I haven't even started the chores yet!"

"Well, hurry. We're waiting for you," everyone shrieked into the phone.

Maurice, with too much New Year's Eve under his belt, was having trouble getting launched. The men dealt with this the only way they knew. They struggled back into their coats, boots, hats and mittens and bustled out the door into the storm to drive to Maurice's to force him out of bed and make him help (or at least watch) them do his work.

One reason I remember that occasion so clearly is that Renaud returned with his coat shredded from backing into the ventilating fan up in the hayloft of the barn. I never did find out what he was doing up there, unless it was to assist brother-in-law Claude, who climbed out a roof hatch of the barn and, despite blizzard conditions, insisted on walking the ridgepole.

Later, back at the house, New Year's continued with supper, then opening gifts under the tree. The children, after ripping their gifts open and hiding them so they wouldn't get broken by the other children, stumbled around looking flushed, unhappy, whiney and tired, until they collapsed on the coat pile in the bedroom.

After the tissue paper and ribbons were cleared away, everyone gathered around the piano to sing. In the beginning I expected traditional English holiday songs, perhaps sung in French. It would have been easier with familiar melodies. But these songs were beyond my ken: *"La Boîteuse," "Chevaliers de la table ronde"* and *"Le Curé de chez nous."*

Renaud sang happily along, taking my hand and urging me to stand at the piano with him and sing along, too. He thought that I could, if I put my mind to it. He didn't realize how overwhelmed I was by all this noise and strangeness, how alone and how despairing I felt about ever fitting in with his family.

The evening progressed from singing to a loud argument between Maurice and sister Carmen, quickly settled with a roar of laughter and an embrace. Then the story telling started.

Renaud sat down next to me, explaining that Maurice had been late because he'd celebrated New Year's Eve too much the night before and hadn't started home until 7:00 *A.M.* Alone, and driving his son Serge's car, he'd taken a left turn too soon and ended up on the cemetery road instead of the St. Charles Road where he lived. After inching along for a few puzzled minutes, he realized that he couldn't sort things out. Stopping the car, he turned off the engine and dozed off to sleep.

But Serge's car had a plastic skeleton dangling from the rear-view mirror, and as Maurice slowly opened his eyes when the cold woke him as dawn lightened the sky, the first sight he saw was that skeleton — entirely out of perspective in view of the background of rows of tombstones and monuments in the local cemetery. "Chris' . . ." said Maurice as, pale and shaking, he joined Renaud in recounting the tale. "Sonofabitch, that skeleton was coming right at me. I thought for sure I was finished!"

Then Renaud and Maurice told me about the time Serge phoned his older brother, Jeannot, at three-thirty one morning, saying that he didn't know what was wrong with his car, but he couldn't get it started. He needed help.

Jeannot grumbled, but got dressed, threw booster cables into his car, a few tools, a flashlight, a can of gas, just in case, and set out toward the stretch of highway near the small town of Ste. Barbe, eight miles away.

And sure enough, there was Serge, waiting by the side of the road, but whether he knew what was wrong with his car or not, he certainly forget to tell his brother on the phone that one reason he couldn't get it started might have been because it was upsidedown in the ditch.

As the family expanded, the tradition of visiting neighbors was replaced by taking turns Happy New Yearing all through the month of January at one relative's home after the other, until the women got tired of having company and rebelled. Then, just as I was beginning to breathe easier around the holiday season, the after-New Year's sorties were replaced by a new and more volatile development. Winter Carnivals.

Quebec City Winter Carnival time is famous all over the north country — like New Orleans' Mardi Gras but cold, and throughout the province, every village and hamlet welcomes the arrival of *Bon'homme Carnival* with open arms. In St. Anicet, the first Winter Carnival was launched with a special church service, assisted by *Bon'homme Carnival* himself, complete with imported drum and bugle band (and glockenspiel). After Mass, the band and a parade of floats rigged out by local organizations and businesses, hayride farm sleds, horses and cutters and snowmobiles, circled the village streets.

Now the St. Anicet Winter Carnivals last from Friday through Sunday and include such friendly sports as broomball, hockey and tug-of-war. On Saturday night dozens of snowmobiles leave the school parking lot and snake across cornfields onto the lake ice in a torch-lit parade, turning and twisting their glowing, serpentine way in a random, follow-the-leader pattern until they reach the local watering hole, where there's a bean supper with pancakes and grillade, followed by a dance.

I liked the warm, friendly French Canadian milieu right from the start. But it never seemed to let up. The Winter Carnival — three days of cheering, fighting the weather, slipping on ice while keeping track of kids, wet mittens and soggy scarves — could scarcely be called a relaxing time. Especially since Renaud (who swore he needed a minimum of eight hours' sleep a night and was always too tired to go to a show in town) suddenly acquired unbelievable stamina during Carnival.

Even after we'd been married more than a dozen holiday seasons, I had trouble getting used to Renaud's extreme friendliness at that time of year. I like to be friendly, too, up to a point, but there were times when my festive-spirit supply could not fill the demand. That's what happened one stormy New Year's when the family gathering had swollen to such proportions that they had to rent a hall in Valleyfield for the occasion.

Everyone came, in spite of the severity of the storm. Though some got anxious and left early, no amount of anxiety on my part could peel Renaud away from his good time. It was only when the bulk of the company gave up at around 2:00 A.M. and headed out the door that Renaud changed his mind and we got ourselves and the children into boots, coats and hats, and high-stepped through the deep snow to our car.

Edging the car carefully through the uncleared roads toward St. Anicet, twenty miles away, Renaud was cheerful and confident. I was worried. We were making deep tracks. I expected any minute to find that we couldn't get through. A mile down the road we saw two men inspecting their stuck car in front of a large snowdrift. It was a situation Renaud couldn't resist. Feeling it his bounden duty to do something helpful, he pulled over.

The children and I shivered in the blast of cold air that swept in through the open window as Renaud leaned out to offer his help. The men refused, saying everything was under control.

Being in a fine mood of "Gladly-die-for-you-ol'-pal," toward these strangers, Renaud wouldn't believe them and said, "I can't just drive off and leave you like this."

The men stopped kicking snow away from their tires and told Renaud that a third member of their party had gone in search of a shovel from a nearby house. They said they would be on their way in no time.

"It's nothing," said Renaud. "Don't worry. I'll just give you a little push."

"No, no, no," the men insisted. "We don't need any help."

Apparently they were going to get it anyway, because Renaud said he wouldn't dream of leaving them half off the road like that — almost into a big snowbank. No, Sir!

"I'll just give you a little push and we'll have you out of there right away," he called reassuringly. Closing his window, and starting the car, he advanced determinedly toward their vehicle as the men moved aside helplessly and we made contact with their bumper, ramming their car the rest of the way into a seven-foot snowdrift. Renaud had done his good deed for the day.

"I guess it didn't work," he said solemnly. "Sorry, fellows. I tried." Off we went as the men went to call a tow truck and their friend emerged from the house with a now useless shovel.

Renaud, who had done his well-intentioned best, couldn't understand my looks of reproach and the children's bursts of explosive laughter all the way home.

* * * * ○ * * * *

PART THREE

Who's Boss Anyway?

* * * * ○ * * *

CHAPTER 18

Self-Employed

Because we started with nothing — less than nothing really, because of car payments and payments to Household Finance — we had to focus on survival of the business over survival of creature comforts.

Renaud did his part by squeezing every bit of worth out of the equipment he bought. Our trucks were patched, and sometimes the patches were patched.

I worked at being thrifty, too, but the business was a greedy monster that was never satisfied with the cream off the top. It wanted the whole thing.

Carried too far, being thrifty can make you crazy. At first, struggling with our finances was almost fun, because we were young, together and had purpose. It wasn't so much fun when we had hot dogs three times a week for supper, my only pair of shoes was held together with masking tape and our three handkerchiefs and two dish towels had patches. Our personal needs, though simple, were persistent. We were raising a family, and it didn't sit well with me that we had to do without a new towel that cost about $5.00, because the business needed something that cost $50,000.00. Renaud and I were giving, giving, giving and the business was taking, taking, taking.

Nothing was easy. I remember thinking about the story of the fellow standing on shore looking at his wife and child being swept out to sea and having to decide which one he would save because he wouldn't have strength to save both. I knew, I just knew, that if the business were out there, too, going under perhaps for the third time, the kid and I wouldn't stand a chance.

After ten years of financial stress, I said, with a tinge of hysteria in my voice, "I don't suppose we could get away for a little holiday."

"Holiday?" Renaud asked. "What for? Why, city people pay plenty to come out to the lake to places just like ours for their summer holidays. Just look at this view, just look at the lake. You couldn't find a better vacation spot anywhere. Besides, we have to expand the shelving in the parts department."

The squeaky wheel gets the oil and no matter what was needed at home, the business was the loudest, squeakiest wheel in the whole world. Still, there was, after all, progress to prove that it made a difference.

Renaud re-invested everything but his small salary. He brought his brother Yves into the business as chief mechanic and partner. They bought more bulldozers, shovels, pavers and dump trucks and a gravel pit. They bought the barn and hop kiln from their father, converting them to offices and garage. They diversified into farm equipment sales and services while still keeping the construction business going at full tilt.

They welded, bought a compressor, jack-hammer and Steam Jenny. They sold farm equipment, lawnmowers, bailer twine and, in the early days, even snowmobiles, bathtubs and lawn chairs. In summer they paved roads, crushed stone, loaded sand and gravel, and they dug.

They dug basements, canals, ditches and graves. In winter

they brought the equipment back to the garage for overhaul and cleaning, and laid off the operators.

Because our employees were local, the business was an extension of home and community. We knew our men not only as employees, but also as friends and neighbors — closeness which generated a new genre of storytelling. Stories about Ralph, who tried to loosen a bolt on the bulldozer one day and called T'coun from across the garage to come hold a chisel against the bolt.

T'coun came willingly. "Be careful," he cautioned Ralph. "That's my hand there."

"Don't worry," said Ralph. "I know what I'm doing."

T'coun grasped the bolt; Ralph swung the hammer and brought it down on T'coun's thumb.

"Why don'cha watch what yer doing?" T'coun screamed in anguish.

"Aw, never mind," laughed Ralph. "Here, hold the chisel with the other hand. We'll get it this time."

"Are you *crazy*?" asked T'coun, backing away.

"Naw," said Ralph. "Come on. I'll be extra careful."

T'coun tucked his aching thumb out of the way and seized the chisel with his good hand. Ralph swung the hammer down and T'coun took off on the warpath as the second thumb suffered the same fate as the first.

Then there was Alex who came for a new spark plug for the chainsaw. He installed it, started it up to make sure it was O.K., set it in the trunk of the car, still running, then slammed the lid. Realizing what he had done, he quickly unlocked the trunk and stopped the chainsaw before it did much damage.

Autumn was in the air when the light in the trunk of *my* car failed. Though it was a minor matter, Renaud said, "Bring it to the garage and leave it. Alex will look at it this afternoon."

It was while he was locking the door at closing time that Renaud heard a faint call for help from the direction of the parking lot. He traced it to the trunk of my car. "Who's there?" Renaud asked.

"It's me," said Alex. "You wouldn't have a flashlight with you, would you?"

"No," Renaud answered. "Why?"

"It's dark in here," said Alex.

"What are you doing in there anyway?" asked Renaud.

"I'm trying to see what's wrong with the light that it don't work," said the muffled voice. "I thought I could get a better idea if I was inside the trunk, but doggone it, then I pulled the lid closed to see if it might be the switch. But, my Gawd, when the lid's closed, I can't see nawthing. And I can't get out."

"O.K. I'll get you out," said Renaud. "Aaahhh . . . say, Alex where's the key?"

"In my pocket," said Alex.

So it was back to the garage to get a crowbar . . .

It was three o'clock on a Sunday morning when Arthur, our grader operator and one of our most loyal employees, pounded on the front door.

Struggling out of a sound sleep, Renaud and I tip-toed in the dark to the living room window, parted the curtain and peered out. A dim figure lurked in the shadows of the cedar by the door. A dark car stood at the top of the driveway. The pounding continued. Finally Renaud called out, "Who's there?"

The pounding stopped. "Who's there?" Renaud repeated.

"Who else?" drawled a sonorous voice. "It's me — Arthur."

Renaud opened the door. I put the kettle on for coffee, and Arthur sat down heavily at the kitchen table.

"I ran out of cigarettes," Arthur said to Renaud, hiccupping gently. "Do you have any cigarettes?"

I had quit smoking again and said so. "Here, have a cigar," said Renaud.

"Nope," said Arthur thickly. "Gotta have a cigarette."

"We don't have any, Arthur," I said.

I put a cup of coffee in front of him. He slopped some cognac into it from a small flask. "I'll drink it," he said. "But I don't want coffee. Want cigarettes."

"No cigarettes here, Arthur," said Renaud.

"Well, O.K. then," said Arthur. "I'll go to the hotel and get some."

"Go home to bed, Arthur," said Renaud. "The hotel's closed."

"Yeah, I know it is," Arthur opined, finishing his coffee and getting unsteadily to his feet. "I been there."

"So you go home and get some sleep, eh, Arthur? You can get cigarettes in the morning," said Renaud.

"Want some tonight," Arthur insisted, chuckling as he headed for the door. "An I'm gonna get some." The door snapped shut. We watched from the window as Arthur maneuvered his way out of the driveway and headed down the highway.

"Do you think he'll go home?" I asked Renaud.

"Oh, of course he will," said Renaud.

I locked the door, put the cups in the sink, turned off the light and we went back to bed.

The next morning we heard that Arthur had tried to get into the hotel his own way — by opening the door with his chainsaw.

Our business is demanding. It's full of frustrations, crowded schedules, untimely breakdowns and emergencies. It is also a money-eater as payroll, inventory, insurance, fuel, power, telephone — an endless line of expenses — swallows everything that comes in.

As Renaud put it one morning when weighted down by expenses and I unwisely mentioned Christmas shopping:

"Do you *know* what it costs every morning for me to just go down there, unlock the door and walk into the garage?"

He meant overhead, but seven-year-old Joey took him literally and thought about the matter all day at school. At supper he proposed his solution to his father. "Papa," he said excitedly, "If it costs that much to unlock the door and walk into the office every morning, why don't you go in through the window?"

If only it were that easy.

"How can you stand it?" I asked Renaud after a harrowing week during which our mechanic caught fire in the grease pit, a customer backed his truck into the fuel pump and the construction crew found a dead stranger in our wheelbarrow on the job site.

"You buy expensive machines and they break down, are vandalized or fall apart, and by the time they're paid for, they're finished," I said. "You buy a truck and an older one collapses; you take a long-term contract at a firm price and wages shoot up; you finish a contract and the fellow who hired you can't pay.

"Customers call you any time of the day or night. Even Sundays. Like last week when that fellow called you to open up and get him a $5.00 part, complained about the price and charged it.

"You try out a bulldozer, buy it at auction and when you get it on the job, find that it burns off a gallon of oil an hour.

"The float falls apart just when you need it most; you buy a second-hand Gradall and the first day on the job, after you leave it parked for the night, someone breaks every window and light on it.

"How can you take it?" I asked. "Why do you stay with a business where, whenever one thing goes right, two thing go wrong?"

Renaud sat silently, reflectively rubbing a calloused hand over his stubble of beard, then summed up the frustration of his long years in business. "I guess the only reason I can think of," he said, "is to find out what the hell's going to happen next!"

* * * * ○ * * * *

CHAPTER 19

Who's Calling?

I stayed home after Billy was born. Not because we could afford to have me stay home during the financial crises nipping at our heels, but because Renaud always insisted, "No wife of mine is going to work." It was an attitude I didn't quarrel with at the time, because no matter how handy or essential a second salary would have been, Renaud would have thought I had poor maternal instincts if I paid a babysitter while I combed my hair, dressed up nice and went to work in a quiet office.

The only responsibility I had toward our business at that time was being kind to Renaud so he could work sixteen hours a day. Being kind to Renaud included taking telephone messages because we couldn't afford to have a secretary, or even a separate telephone, for the business.

Taking telephone messages was not as easy as it sounds, partly because of the language problem and partly because most callers didn't want to leave messages.

"Any calls for me while I was at work?" Renaud asked.

"No," I said. "Well, there was one call."

"Who was it?"

"I don't know."

"You don't know?"

"No."

"Didn't you even ask? It might have been important."

"Of course I asked. They didn't say. They hung up. If it's important, they'll call back."

A few seconds of silence.

"Who did it sound like?"

"What?"

"The person who called. Was it a man or a woman?"

"A man."

"French or English?"

"English. I think. Well, I don't know. He could have been French and speaking English."

"Did he have an accent?"

"He didn't say enough for me to be able to tell."

"Who did he ask for?"

"He asked for you, of course."

"No, I mean did he ask for me as Mr. Caza or as Renaud?"

"Gee . . . I think he asked, 'Is your husband there?'"

"Did he say he'd call back?"

"No, he just hung up."

"Why didn't you ask for his name, or his phone number, or ask him to call back in an hour or two?"

"I did. I mean, I tried. I told you. He hung up."

A merciful pause. About twenty seconds. Then . . .

"Did it sound like Pierre?"

"Huuuhh?"

"The person calling — did it sound like Pierre?"

"No, I don't think it was him."

"Could it have been Ken?"

"Nooo, I'm sure it wasn't him."

"Gaetan?"

"No."

The rest of the evening was pretty quiet. Then, as we were getting ready for bed, Renaud reminded me that he had been awake since six that morning (I knew — I had been there, too, fixing his breakfast and letting the dog and cat in and out, in and out and trying to be quiet so the baby would sleep a bit longer). He said that he had put in a punishing day watching machinery fall apart and listening to customers say, "I bought the same part five years ago and it only cost $9.00 then." He said that surely it was not too much to expect that one's wife, sitting at home all day with nothing to do but watch television and look after the minor needs of three pre-school children, could take a simple telephone message.

Feeling outraged, yet guilty, if such a combination of feelings is possible, I grumbled that I'd like to see him keep someone from hanging up if he's a mind to. But Renaud's frustration strengthened my resolve to get it right next time.

When Renaud left for work the next morning, I put pen and pad on the telephone table. I was ready. Nobody would get by me this time without at least some useful clue slipping out. The stage was set; determination was high. The telephone rang:

"Is Mr. Caza there?" Clue number one, they called him Mr. Caza. Good start.

"I'm sorry," I said. "He isn't here right now." Adding quickly, "Could I take a mess . . . "

"Bzzzz . . ."

Now, you might suggest, why didn't I first ask who was calling? But to ask "Who's calling?" before telling the caller that Renaud is not home sounds suspiciously as though he's trying to avoid that particular person. It goes like this:

"Is Mr. Caza there?"

"Who's calling please?"

"This is Mr. Scrounge."

"I'm sorry, he's not in right now."

See what I mean? Sounds as though he's just not in for Mr. Scrounge. While that might be O.K. for big, impersonal business operations, in a small outfit like ours it's better public relations to say first that Renaud isn't at home and take a chance on getting information.

Later the telephone rang again.

"Is Renaud there?" A-ha — Renaud this time.

"I'm expecting him any minute. Can I have him call you?"

"No thanks, I'll ring back later."

"Would you leave me your name, please?"

"No, never mind, I'll call again."

"But . . ."

"Buuzzzz . . ."

Again! I tapped the unused pen on the blank notepad. Of course, I could say there were no calls, but if I did, the caller might stop at the garage later and tell Renaud that he'd called the house. And how would that sound if I'd already said there were no calls? Right. It would sound sneaky.

The solution to this dilemma? Aside from burying my head in the laundry hamper whenever the telephone rings, I didn't find one, until the business got its own telephone. We still get business calls at home, but now I just tell them the office number and Renaud is so busy answering the phone at work that he never asks me if anyone called.

Around here the telephone is a mixed blessing. When we first moved to the cottage, with two small boys, we took the precaution of ordering a wall-mounted phone, which was installed between the kitchen and living room, well above toddler reach.

That meant there was no privacy and no getting away from household noise while talking on the phone. With its short cord, it also meant that I couldn't reach the stove when something boiled over or rescue the cat from the dog or stop the bottle of Kool-Aid from crashing to the floor. The situation was not ideal, but at least we always knew where the telephone was.

Then one day, about ten years later, I had the old phone removed from the wall as an anniversary gift and ordered a desk phone with the longest cord possible. That's when our troubles began, because while it enabled me to pass the phone directly to the bedridden, do all manner of useful household tasks while talking (turning hamburgers, scrubbing the bathroom sink, cleaning the stove and even washing dishes) there were still disadvantages, such as pacing the floor waiting for an expected call, then staring incredulously as some tousle-headed small child, who had been tying up the line for goodness knows how long, wandered out of a bedroom with the phone.

Then there was the customer who stopped by the house and could hardly wait to tell us that he had called earlier and asked to speak to Renaud. Linda, five years old, had answered. Never one to drag out the business of telephone conversations (at least not at that point) and not wanting to admit that she didn't understand his brisk French delivery, she simply said, "I don't speak English; I don't speak French; I only speak Spanish," and hung up.

A few years later, when Billy was away at John Abbott College, he tried to make a collect call home to us. His room at the dorm was on the top floor and the pay phone was at ground level, down a series of twists and turns of corridors and stairways. Making this long journey with his coin, Bill dialed the operator, who rang the house, and Linda answered. "Will you accept the charges on a collect call from Mr. Bill Caza?" The operator asked.

Linda, ever firm in her dealings, said, "He's not here, he's away at school," and hung up, leaving an enraged brother dangling from the other end of the dead line.

* * * * ○ * * * *

CHAPTER 20

O.K., Bernie, Cut That Out!

We didn't know what adjustments would have to be made in our marriage, or who would make them, but we figured that if we were in accord with attitudes about important things, such as honesty, integrity, the Golden Rule and fidelity, everything else would be easy.

The only trouble is, we neglected to put forth so much as a tentative feeler on such drab things as attitudes about how often I get the car, who puts out the garbage, who lets the dog and cat in and out, in and out, in and out, and who gets up for the 2:00 A.M. feeding.

It didn't take long to realize that marriage should be a college credit course involving much research, perhaps even apprenticeship, in order to deal with the dumb, frustrating and outrageous things that fill the days of family living. It was an eye-opener for me, because I don't remember life being so complicated in my parents' home. Back then, day followed smooth day, and rough spots, if there were any, were sanded away by other hands — not mine.

It was only after Renaud and I married that I discovered what it meant to be a wife — or should I say what it didn't mean.

It didn't mean discussing the state of the nation's business, the justice of certain government legislation or even the latest weather report. It meant, instead, facing such unanswerable questions as: why I let us run out of eggs, gas, clean socks, milk, beer, Raisin Bran, toilet paper or postage stamps. Or why the pump isn't running, or why it won't stop running all the time. Or why I put the thermal knits in the dryer instead of hanging them over the chair backs to dry, and now they won't fit anyone — with the possible exception of the dog.

Being married meant a lot of explaining of things that I didn't think I should have to explain, such as why I'm messing about with paint and plaster or ceramic tiles or wallpaper, instead of doing something useful, like washing the car or shovelling snow from the driveway.

Being married meant apologizing for a mosquito waking us at 4:00 A.M. and being asked why *I* let it into the house so it is *bzooming* and *bzzzoinging* around the room. Heaven knows he needs his sleep, Renaud says, and I sympathize with him, but after all, it isn't *my* mosquito or I would give it a name and simply shout, O.K., Bernie, cut that out!"

I discovered that being in a bilingual television viewing area could have been culturally stimulating if the networks had been smart enough not to cast top-rated French channel shows opposite top-rated English shows. After a long day of work Renaud felt entitled to the comedic relief of his program, while I, after a day of chasing babies, wanted mine.

Renaud, as bread winner, won most of the time anyway, and when he did, I was cross; he was self-righteous and we were both disappointed in each other.

If marriage itself didn't bring enough discoveries, there was the matter of parenthood, which introduced us to such entertainments as rounding up escapes from the ant farm bust-out, chasing after sleepwalking children determined to swim in the lake in the winter and retrieving the hamster from the dog's mouth. It meant comforting horrified Joey after he'd squashed a big blueberry when running across the kitchen barefoot and thought it was a crisp-n-squishy bug. It meant coaxing the cat out of the tree house and cleaning up the mess after Billy found a tube of black powdered dye, spilled it over the counter, sink and floor and tried to clean it up with wet rags — compounding the problem. And I won't soon forget the time I had to put on an appropriately appreciative smile at the sight of a car that had been given four generous coats of liquid self-polishing floor wax in the hot sun by a resident Boy Scout bent on doing his good deed for the day.

But of all these shockers, one of the biggest disappointments of married life was my discovery that I was not a good housekeeper. French Canadian women are fantastic housekeepers. They scrub, polish and paint everything. All the women I met in my new surroundings had some kind of household magic that dealt with mess with vigor and determination, leaving everything super clean and orderly.

I used to believe that if I had enough storage space, I could deal with housework, but my mother-in-law had had a bigger house to care for, eight children and less storage space, yet there was never any clutter. I tried to be like her and keep my house in order, but I had too many projects that created piles of clay, messy paint tubes, stiffened brushes, reams of paper and puffs of cotton batting — and I also had a heavy schedule of Cubs, Brownies and P.T.A.

Mrs. Caza didn't have projects, but she had five hundred chickens, a fifty-by-fifty-foot garden and a demanding family. When it came to housekeeping, she had me beat by a country mile.

Still, I didn't marry Renaud because I had an insatiable yearning to scrub and cook, and he didn't marry me because he needed complications in his life. It made me wonder why a man brought up in a community where every housewife qualified for a gold medal for neat-and-clean, would go out, find, pursue, marry and bring back into home territory a wife of different language, background and religion, who had no idea how to run a household.

Take the matter of laundry, for instance. Some housewives work hard to make their laundry bright. When their white linens become dingy and bleach no longer works, they hide them out of sight by hanging them in the basement, sticking them in the dryer or tearing them up for dust rags rather than hanging them out on the clothesline next to their truly-whites.

I prefer to hang my grey linens boldly on the line, with only a slight qualm, as my conscience is soothed by the fact that our water is iron-hard. Then when I buy a new pack of T-shirts for Renaud or the boys, or brand-new, dazzling white handkerchiefs (they won't use tissues), I hide them on indoor lines for the first few washings, until they mellow to meet the grey standard and can take their place on the outside line with everything else.

I tried to be a good housekeeper, especially when I saw that it was expected of me. I went to extra lengths when Renaud phoned one afternoon to say that he was bringing Aunt Cécile and Aunt Aldea home in twenty minutes.

Although I wasn't good at organization, over the years I became accomplished at the housewife's sprint. Moving quickly and methodically, I raced from one end of the house to the other, throwing jackets and boots into closets, polishing jam from the refrigerator door, turning cushions on the sofa to the fresh side, sweeping beach sand out the door, whisking fingerprints off the windows, dusting and polishing exposed surfaces and stepping out of my slob clothes and into a neat blouse and skirt.

I may have been out of breath and a bit red in the face when Aunt Cécile and Aunt Aldea came through the doorway, but by God, I had beat the clock.

CHAPTER 21

* * * * ○ * * * *

Food for Thought

The clearest memory I have of Renaud's family is the first time I was invited to Sunday dinner. "Invited" is hardly the right word. Sunday dinner at the Caza's was always open house, with everyone welcome.

What seemed like dozens of Cazas of all ages, talked, laughed and milled about. I didn't understand a word, but with such cheer and activity I was busy taking it all in.

At the table, Renaud sat on my right, his father to my left at the head of the table, and his mother at the foot of the table, close to the stove and serving counter. Everyone else sat wherever they wanted.

I didn't know what to expect of the meal, nor was I apprehensive, but when Renaud's father tucked into his plate I wasn't sure I could go on. Swimming in a pale white sauce with large globules of yellow fat floating on top was mashed potatoes, corn, a portion of chicken thigh and two boiled chicken feet. I didn't begrudge him his Sunday treat, but it was daunting to sit next to him and watch him eat those boiled chicken feet, sucking at them like straws, one toe at a time, to get all the juices, while rivulets of grease ran down the creases from the corners of his mouth to his chin. I was glad the rest of us weren't served that delicacy. Marriage into

115

this family, which was pretty far from my mind at the time anyway, became even more distant.

Subsequent meals at Renaud's home leaned strongly toward rich sauces and a lot of fat. Most popular were *patte à cochon* (pig's knuckles), *ragout boulette, tourtière*, beans, soups rich in fat and pies with crusts so rich they were almost transparent. I was also introduced to macaroni salads. I'm not a pasta fan, and the combining of slithery, cold macaroni with heavy dollops of mayonnaise was more than I could bear.

The Caza table, however, held many delightful surprises: molasses pie, thin pancakes with home-produced maple syrup and toast made by mashing slices of bread onto a hot lid of the wood stove and turning it over with a spatula until it was crisp, somewhat charred and delicious.

As our relationship became more serious, I wondered what Renaud would think of my cooking, which was more along the lines of lean pot roasts, lots of vegetables, salads, fatless soups, Chinese stir-fry and rice and fresh fruit salads.

When I discussed the cooking issue with Renaud, about the time we got engaged, he shrugged it off lightly, assuring me that he couldn't care less what kind of cook I was. That was comforting, except that the reason he considered it unimportant was because he was still living and eating at home and didn't know what I was talking about.

Before marriage, I didn't worry about food or cooking. When I went to work, I had meals at home with my parents; when I took a job out of town, meals were at the boarding house where I lived; in Greenland, there was the mess hall.

Even after Renaud and I were married, for a couple of years, meals were routine and un-noteworthy. Often we ate at restaurants because we were both working. At home we ate a lot of canned soup, grilled cheese sandwiches and store cookies. We visited our families and ate with them on weekends.

With time I learned to make a lot of the traditional specialties of French Canada, but I left out most of the fat so I could eat them, too.

I don't remember when things got out of control, but there was the business with its awkward hours, then children, and being broke. It all contributed.

Mostly, I think, it had to do with being a parent. There was not only the continuous cycle of meals, but all the refereeing as the children grew more assertive. With their help mealtime was often reduced to a contest without rules.

"You got a bigger bowl of Jell-O than I did!"

"No, I didn't. *Yours* is bigger."

"It is not."

"Oh yeah? Do you wanna trade?"

"Heck no, you breathed on it."

"I did not!"

"You did too. You blew germs all over it."

"I didn't!"

"You did!"

"Didn't!"

"Did!"

"Mommmm . . ."

So I, in my wisdom, was supposed to decide which Jell-O was bigger, better and more germ-free, then choose which favorite child is to get said bigger, better and more germ-free Jell-O.

Or:

"You had six cookies."

"I didn't. I had five."

"I saw you sneak one when you thought no one was looking."

"I didn't."

"You did!"

"Didn't!"

"Did!"

"Mommm . . ."

Then there was: "You didn't spend your lunch money on the meal today at school. I saw you get three jelly donuts, a piece of pie and a soft drink."

"Tattle tale! What about the time I saw you getting four servings of French fries instead of the meal?"

"Aw, that's different, the meal wasn't good that day. They just had fried maggots" (their name for cafeteria-style fried rice).

Then there's breakfast, when they have to protect themselves from each other's evil eye in a private paranoia that if someone looks in their direction their dish will be contaminated.

They arrange cereal box barricades between each other. Ketchup bottles and syrup jugs are lined up and arms curved protectively around their plates to ensure more privacy. The tone of the meal is set by:

"Mom, he's looking at me!"

I say, "Eat your breakfast."

"But Mom, he's doing it on *purpose*!"

"Uummmm . . . Eat your breakfast."

"Look! See? He's doing it again!"

"What? Who? When? Mom, I didn't do *anything*!"

"You did too, and you *coughed*! You coughed right at me!"

"I was just clearing my throat a bit."

"Don't think I don't know you're trying to make me mad. I saw you smile!"

"Mom! He touched that piece of toast and took a different one. I'm not going to eat a piece of toast *he* touched."

Then I say wistfully, "I wish a total stranger would walk in right now." (They're always nice in front of total strangers.)

Or sometimes they wander around on a dull day, looking hopeless and folorn: "Mom, I'm hungry."

"Then get something to eat."

"What is there?"

"There's plenty of bread. You can make toast, or have a sandwich. There's cheese, peanut butter, jam, honey, bologna or cereal. There's cold ham, oranges, potato salad and cocoa."

"Aw . . . Gee, how come we never have anything good to eat around here? I could starve to death!"

Within a few years, my entire life revolved around doing laundry, caring for husband, caring for children, caring for pets, caring for house, coping with the local watering hole, the business and local talent, and dealing with the challenge of always having to get another meal on the table.

Renaud came home for lunch every day, and as I was waving goodbye to him from the living room window, I was mentally reviewing the contents of the pantry and freezer to decide what to make for supper.

Only a person who really dislikes cooking would bother figuring out that there are 1,095 meals a year. That's a lot of meal planning, shopping, cooking and dirty dishes.

For a long time I felt it my duty to be a good cook. I thought it was important that my little family work up a passion about "Mom's cooking." But it was no use. If I served something twice in the same week — which happens often because I tend to cook in quantity and count on leftovers — they would say, "Why do you always make the same old stuff? We never get anything different to eat around here! I'm so tired of spaghetti" or "Not turkey, again!"

Even the children's visiting friends were a problem. If I served cabbage rolls to a young friend and he didn't know what they were and didn't want to find out, he ate peanut butter sandwiches or Corn Flakes, while I got exasperated looks from my children.

Even if I did come through with something great, like pot roast and baked potato, I held my tongue graciously when one of their friends said, sotto voce, to my kids, "Not bad, but you should taste the way *my* mom makes it!" Yeah well . . .

Cooking aside, the kitchen was the busiest room in the house. Here the children did their homework, built toothpick forts and popsicle-stick towers. Here I sewed, mended and patched. Here we removed splinters, inserted ear drops, applied bandages and resolved conflicts. It was busy, noisy, and crowded. Sometimes I thought that everything was stored in our busy kitchen and avalanching kitchen cupboards, which left little room for dishes.

"Excuse me," I would say, getting up to wash the soup bowls so they could be used later for dessert. It was the same routine with knives and spoons. Of course, it was all very rustic, but I still thought it was carrying the pioneering spirit too far when I had to jump up and wash dishes and utensils between courses.

There was never enough room for everything — especially since housewives who live in deep country spend all their free time filling shelves and freezer against being stuck without a car or being snowed in. From rhubarb to squash season, Renaud could expect, any time he came home, to find boxes, crates and baskets of fiddleheads, strawberries, beets, carrots, cucumbers, tomatoes or corn, all waiting their turn to be stacked in freezer or jar. "You have to get these things in season," I would explain, but this did not appear to console him as he hop-scotched over the perishable inventory on his way to the fridge. He, of course, shook his head and moaned, "Why? Why . . ."

In general, Renaud has been patient about my cooking. He can put up with a lot before finally telling me that if there's anything he can't stand it's creamed peas on toast or smoked cod more than once a year. I even go overboard on his favorite regional recipes. Once I get the hang of how to prepare them,

I get carried away and serve them time and again until he has to let me know it's enough.

I have no desire to excel in the kitchen, though. In fact, my main ambition is to slide by inconspicuously. I've always found that with a couple of dependable specialties, people overlooked what I couldn't do and appreciated what I could do. So I learned to make a smooth gravy, assemble a creditable chicken pot pie, bake my own bread and make a great welsh rarebit and a fine rice custard.

Renaud doesn't have any cooking skills. He can boil water if he has to, but would rather not. Sometimes, though, he has to shift for himself. Like when I was in the hospital having Billy, and Renaud had nothing but bologna and mustard sandwiches and coffee for the whole week. "It was the only thing I knew how to make," he confessed.

Then take eggs. There were a lot of rules and regulations surrounding Renaud's breakfast egg. It had to be sunny side up, with just the right degree of firmness, and the yolk could not be broken.

One morning, as Renaud was saying, "Please be careful with my egg," I rebelled. I didn't have time to hover protectively over the thing. I had ten other things to do, so I handed the egg to him, put the frying pan on the stove, turned on the burner and told him that since he was so smart, he should go ahead and do it himself.

Renaud strode purposefully to the stove, waited for the pan to get smoky hot, dropped a lump of butter in it and hit the egg on the edge. The pan skittered off the stove and the egg landed with a sizzle on the red-hot burner. Renaud said "Ooops" and smiled apologetically, but I now had eleven other things to do, and I still had to cook the egg.

Which reminds me of the morning, while I was recovering from surgery, that Linda boiled an egg for Renaud's breakfast, cooking it three minutes (from start — in cold water, to finish — in lukewarm water) and tried to remove the shell the way she'd seen me do it with hard-boiled eggs for salad, by smacking it briskly on the counter and rolling it.

Because Renaud's hectic days don't allow much time for meals and I'm never sure if he'll be home early or late, I have to plan lunches that can be ready within minutes of the car coming into the driveway so he can be out and on his way again within, say, twenty minutes. It's like a drive-in restaurant around here at noontime.

As if that weren't bad enough, an extra male appetite or two occasionally shows up for lunch — with no advance warning. It happens about a dozen times a year and generally follows the same pattern as last time. At about twenty minutes before noon, the phone rang:

"Margie?"

"Yes . . ."

"Uh . . . er . . . do we have any food in the house?"

"I'd be surprised if we didn't."

"Well, these two fellows came from Montreal this morning to fix the bulldozer. I'm bringing them home for lunch. We'll be there in about twenty minutes."

"Uuuhhh . . . Hummmmm?" I responded. Taking this for ecstatic approval rather than shock, Renaud, who never lingers on the phone, signed off before I could tell him that the dog had found a rotting eel in the weeds near shore and I was in the midst of giving him a bath. I raced to the bathroom, let the water out of the tub, rinsed it in a flash while not inhaling any more dead fish smell than necessary and pushed the only slightly cleaner dog into Linda's room, where he alternated rubbing his wet fur on her bedspread and scratching at the door and whining throughout the whole lunch hour.

The hot chicken sandwich I had planned for Renaud

wouldn't stretch far enough for two more, so I revised my meal plan and started the countdown.

- 18 minutes to go: Turn on stove, grab potatoes, peel, cut into small pieces, rinse, get them on the stove. Throw two steaks from freezer to counter.
- 16½ minutes: Get empty box from under pool table. Run into living room, throw all sneakers, sandals, crayons, sand shovels, pails and game pieces into the box. Return box to under pool table.
- 15 minutes: Drag out vacuum cleaner, run it over living room and kitchen, unintentionally sucking up a piece of cucumber and the cat's kibble.
- 14 minutes: Sweep current project (ceramics) off kitchen table and into another cardboard box. Shove box under pool table.
- 13 minutes: Check bathroom sink, soap dish and towels.
- 12 minutes: Empty and wash ashtrays.
- 11 minutes: Make salad.
- 10 minutes: Set plastic container of frozen strawberries in bowl of hot water to thaw.
- 9 minutes: Take handful of rolls out of freezer, and biscuits for shortcake. Throw them in oven. Turn oven on. Get out whipping cream.
- 8 minutes: Set table.
- 7 minutes: Wipe streaks and stains off floor.
- 6 minutes: Wipe streaks and stains off me.
- 5 minutes: Set pan of dirty dishes out of sight in oven.
- 4 minutes: Clear magazines, purse, catalogues, newspapers, pencils and dog biscuits off coffee table. Dust coffee table.
- 3 minutes: Change shirt, brush hair.
- 2 minutes: Make coffee, whip cream, put milk, relish, pickles on table.

- 1 minute: Throw plastic bags of garbage outside back door as car turns into driveway. Throw steaks into hot pan.
- 0 — Blast off: Greet men as they come through the doorway talking, and for the next half-hour serve table and smile.

When they finished eating, the men got up from the table, still talking, put their coats on, still talking, and left the house with an offhand "Thanks." I turned back to the kitchen feeling unappreciated and sorry for myself. I remembered the dog, let him out of Linda's room and changed her bed. I re-washed the dog. Then there was still the table to clear and dishes to wash and, oh no, it was time to cook supper. Men, bah! Meals, humbug!

CHAPTER 22

* * * * ○ * * * *

Who's Boss?

There were enough things to adjust to in marriage without adding a power struggle. But it was there.

Before we were married, I couldn't find a single attitude in Renaud that would have caused me to think we were not equal.

"Maybe I'll work after we're married."

"Sure . . . Fine. O.K."

"We'll share the housework."

"Sure . . . Fine. O.K."

When we go into business, we'll be there together."

"Sure . . . Fine. O.K."

"Perhaps we'll have children."

"Sure . . . Fine. O.K."

I was naïve enough to look forward to marriage making us closer. It did, but that closeness itself created problems. On the other hand, if closeness on a daily basis is what brings about the husband and wife bonding that makes marriage endure, then I guess we can thank our lucky stars that we had the kind of household where plumbing exploded, dogs threw up on our slippers while feet were still in them and kids needed dental work just when we'd finally earmarked the savings account for a real vacation.

We used to talk about having a fifty-fifty marriage, though

neither of us really knew what that meant. Probably I felt that it meant I would wash the dishes and Renaud would dry them. Renaud clearly thought, in his male, French Canadian heart-of-hearts, that fifty-fifty meant that he would make all the important decisions and I would make all the ones that didn't really matter. It was frustrating and humbling to discover that any time I put in my oar and tried to direct the boat, Renaud would jerk it out of my hand and say, "Let's do it my way."

After a while, I realized that the last big decision we'd really shared was our response to the question: "Do you take this man/woman to be your husband/wife?" After that it was every man/woman for him/herself. We were smack dab in the middle of that limbo where women think they have rights but men know better.

I recognized inequality when I saw it, but by the time the ink was dry, I was too busy to haggle about it. Worrying about who had the advantage took too much time and energy, and it killed the incentive to fuss about what was fair and what wasn't.

I respected the fact that Renaud had a demanding job and did it well. So what if he never saw a floor being waxed, never washed a plate or filled a pepper shaker or defrosted a freezer? The only thing that bothered me was that he thought I had things soft at home.

Whenever he stopped by unexpectedly when passing by on business, he usually found me struggling with the garden, cleaning ashes out of the fireplace, hanging wallpaper, sewing, baking or playing with the kids or deeply involved in one of my projects. But there was that time in the middle of the morning . . .

The kids were off at school, the dog had settled on the mat in the kitchen and the cat was curled up on the refrigerator. The sun beamed warmly through the window; the sofa beckoned. I gave in and crawled under the quilted throw for a short nap.

About half an hour later, Renaud, driving by on his way to look at a drainage job, and prodded, no doubt, by some sort of fink sixth sense, decided to stop in for a cup of coffee. Or to check on me.

I didn't hear his car coming into the driveway, because he cut the motor and coasted in. I don't know what he expected to find, but he slipped his key in the front door lock quietly, boots in hand, walking on tip-toe in sock feet. At the first "snick" of the key in the lock, I bounded up and reached for the dish towel that was draping over the arm of the sofa. But it was impossible to appear bright, alert and terribly industrious with the corners of my eyes still stuck together and the pattern of the crochet pillow imprinted in bas relief along the side of one sleep-flushed cheek.

I looked flustered. Guilty. Renaud grinned and said, "I knew it, I *knew* it!" and "Ah-ha! Caught you, eh?" and I was left without a word of defence.

But I've been watching today's women, and I've noticed they don't feel guilty about taking time for themselves. They're a bright lot, with a future limited only by what they want from life. They know where they're going and what they're doing, and they're more in command than any preceding generation. Today's woman are born leaders, with the strength and potential to compete in any profession and raise a family at the same time.

I'm glad to hear that, but I'm not about to apply it to my own situation. I told Renaud about it one night at suppertime, though, because I wanted him to know how smart today's women are. He obviously believed it, too, because he didn't choke on his spaghetti or fall out of his chair or anything dramatic like that. He smiled agreeably, nodded, helped himself to more grated Parmesan cheese, took a sip of coffee, sighed with relief, handed me his big ring of keys and said, "That's wonderful news, dear. I'll get your breakfast tomorrow morning, and you go and take over the business."

Well, that stopped me for a minute, because just reading about today's smart women didn't give me much sense of direction.

I had already figured out that I was not equipped to lead our household, let alone the world, out of chaos. I'm the sort of person who falls apart when lightning hits the tree next to the window I'm sitting at, the toilet backs up or a screaming child comes running up from the beach with a fish hook dangling from an eyelid, and I might as well accept it and forget about such things as running for public office, where I'll be sure to make a fool of myself right there in front of everybody.

Whereas the women of today have the world on a string, what I've got is a tiger by the tail, and at this stage in life I'm rather afraid to let go. These things tend to boomerang, and I doubt that I'd be brave enough to handle the consequences.

Besides, the new breed of woman is better organized. Right from the start, their plans involve independence, self-sufficiency, perhaps a career, maybe one perfect child, a retirement fund and sometimes a husband — if he knows his place. I made plans, too, but so did Renaud, and he definitely knows *his* place — and I'd better not forget it.

So I guess you could say that:

> The Liberated Woman
> Is now the thing to be
> But I was born ten years too soon
> — and it's too late for me!

PART IV

Kids, Pets and Mayhem!

* * * * ○ * * *

CHAPTER 23

Being a Parent
Is a Gradual Thing

To say I was not used to children would be putting it mildly. My sole contact with the diapered generation at the time of our marriage was through a few neighborhood babysitting jobs as a teenager, in the course of which I felt secure in the knowledge that I could handle any emergency, with the possible exception of the baby waking up.

I didn't mention that to Renaud, of course, because I assumed that every young woman was in the same boat, and everyone learned about children as they had them. What I didn't take into consideration was what was expected of me by a husband who'd been brought up in a big family where girls got used to handling babies at an early age. By the time a girl was ten years old, she could not only hold baby brother, sister, cousin or neighbor, but could feed, burp, bathe, change and dress it. And she gained proficiency as she went along, taking the whole business of babies for granted, leading all the male members of the family to think of baby care as an inherited feminine attribute. Apparently the only thing men knew, or needed to know, about babies was that they were another mouth to feed.

How could I, fresh out of the indulgent independence I

enjoyed as a young career woman, be expected to know that keeping a household on an even keel, a husband happy and tending to the needs of babies was not something that came naturally with the solemnization of the marriage vows? Just as there had been nothing to prepare me for the real world of married life, there was even less to prepare me for the raising of three vigorous children.

Consider, if you will, a young couple enjoying dinner at the Golden Steer. Music, candlelight, sweet nothings in the ear. Then, perhaps, window shopping for furniture for their home, dreaming of a future full of romantic evenings in front of the fireplace alone. Together. And ask yourself if it makes sense that the next item on the program is wet diapers, runny noses, spilled pablum and helping put Mr. Potato Head together.

Forget, for the moment, how lovely romance and courtship are, and ask instead about dealing with guppies, dogs, cats, and farms, dirty floors, taking out splinters, cleaning the oven and prying baby fingers from around the barber's nose.

I tell you, I just wasn't prepared for motherhood. In fact, there were a lot of things I wasn't prepared for and it took some strenuous chopping away at the jungle of married life before I could see a glimmer of daylight through the dense brush.

For one thing, it was a shock to discover that being a Mom is not the serene condition shown in magazines, where a calm mother is seated by the fireplace, infant on her lap, while the older offspring gather around and gaze adoringly up at her. Around here, it's frequently every man for himself, and I soon found out that a family of two adults and three children doesn't represent a very good democracy because the children outnumber the adults.

"Let's vote on it," the children would shout eagerly about some outrageous request.

"Can't you guess how it's going to turn out?" I would ask acidly, maintaining my unpopular stand on the issue.

Or I might get caught as a straight-man, like when we had a hot dog barbecue in the backyard and I called loudly and often from the kitchen doorway, warning the impatient children to wait for the embers and not to cook the hot dogs in the flames.

After about the eighth warning, Billy called urgently, "Mom!"

"What?" I asked.

"Don't yell through the screen door," he shouted. And when I fell into his trap and asked "Why?" he chortled, "You'll *strain* your voice."

Parenthood opened up a whole new world of discovery. I discovered that if a parent is dense enough to give a budding young scientist a chemistry set for Christmas, well, that parent had better be prepared to re-paper Joey's bedroom.

I discovered the ingenuity of fifth-graders when Billy had to write five hundred times, "I will not run down the stairs," as homework, because he had been caught doing just that at school. I came into the kitchen to find him at my typewriter, working away industriously, with ten sheets of paper and nine carbons neatly rolled around the cylinder. "At this rate," he said gleefully, "I'll be finished in no time."

Then when we watched hot-doggers do trick skiing on TV, one fellow executed a double-somersault off a quick drop-away.

"Hey", said Billy. "I did that once."

"You did?" I asked in amazement.

"Yeah," he said. "Not on purpose, of course."

I discovered that being a mother means hoping the children will soon be out of diapers and able to get into winter clothing without help and then wishing feverently that they were still babies as I rush to P.T.A., taxi them around, volunteer for Cubs and Brownies and deny them the pleasure of staying up till midnight and living on soft drinks, chips and chocolate bars.

Before long, I was dealing with motherhood the way I dealt with my first encounter with a feather mattress. I clearly remember leaning back on the guest room bed at Mrs. Caza's, only to find myself suddenly staring up at the ceiling as I sank to rock bottom with the ends of the mattress rising up on either side. Getting out was like climbing out of a bowl of raised yeast dough.

Parenthood provided many "feather mattress" situations. I discovered, for instance, that it is not a good idea to bake plastic toys or favors in a birthday cake. Nor is it a good idea to temporarily hide a plastic dishpan of dirty dishes out of sight in the oven. The resultant mess after forgetting and turning the oven on to pre-heat is disgusting.

There was also the train trip to Grandma's with the three children. I forgot the blanket for the baby and Billy got thirsty, trotted up to the bathroom, squirted soap from the dispenser into the paper cup and drank it.

My life was not destined for calm, otherwise why would I say "Go ahead" when Joey took up boxing and wanted to change rooms with Linda so he could have a room of his own to use as a training camp. He wrapped an old mattress around the chimney for a sparring partner, braced a tension chinning bar in the downstairs doorway, filled an old canvas dunnage bag with wet sawdust for a punching bag and went around looking for real contenders.

Linda took the boys' room with the built-in bunks, and Billy took over the family room for his digs. And "digs" was the right word for it, what with all the stuff that was already there, the addition of Bill, a folding cot, his clothes and the fact that the room had no closet, bureau or even a door.

I learned that parents must listen with logic as well as with ears. One day Billy persuaded me to drive him and his coin collection to nearby Huntingdon, where, he said, they had a place to clean coins professionally. I didn't realize until we were parked right there that the sign "Coin Wash" might be ambiguous, but it certainly didn't have anything to do with numismatics.

Involvement with Cubs, Brownies and Scouts meant field trips, cook-outs, scraped knees, father-son banquets, parades, forgotten Cub hats, chartered buses that come late, parents' night performances when skits fall flat and kazoos suffer blow-outs. It also meant getting a flat tire on the long, isolated stretch of the Plank Road at midnight after a costume party for Scouts and Cubs. I had on a wine and gold satin mandarin costume and was accompanied by a pink clown Cub and a brown hot-dog Scout holding a mustard pot, and with the spare tire also flat, I had to stop a passing car for help. Then there was awards night when enthusiastic Cubs and Brownies get seven or eight badges and others get only one and make you feel mean, though you know each got exactly what they worked for.

I also discovered that children are devious, as when they asked, right in front of the visitor they'd brought home for supper, if their friend can stay for the week. "It's all right with his Mom," they insist. What can I do but say, "We'll see, dear," as I administer a quick nudge to my child's foot under the table, change the subject and remind him with narrowed eyes that I have told them at least a million times to always ask me privately first. "Gee, Mom — I forget . . ."

Then there are the questions: such gems as "Does the world weigh more or less now than it did ten or a hundred or a thousand years ago?" Any answer just leads to more questions (Why? How much more/less). And, "If people can emulate sounds of animal language, why can't animals do the same with human words?" and "Since wool shrinks when you wash it, does it also shrink on the sheep when they get caught in the rain?" and if not — "How come?"

I had a few questions, too — such as, Why are children so devastatingly mercurial that they can swing from an enraged and tearful "I don't like you any more" to a sunny, smiling "You're the best Mommie in the whole world"? Or complain because we won't let them get a tattoo, even though "everybody has one" or dye their hair green and purple, and in the next breath say how great we are because we let them sleep on the roof.

Many times I couldn't possibly have won, even if I'd been able to walk on water, which I couldn't. Like the time I bought colonial print wallpaper for the kitchen, spent the day applying it and watched, defeated, as Billy, Joey and Linda came home from school, stood in the doorway, looked around and said, "Ugh!"

Then there were those times Renaud said, "You're too soft with the boys. They get everything their own way," continuing with, "When I was their age . . ." This was all very well, but then when I got cross and scolded them, Renaud would look accusingly at me over his lowered newspaper and launch gently into the bit about "Weren't *you* ever young?" or "They're only kids once, you know."

Ah, but the time I won't forget was when I complained because the business was so demanding that Renaud and I seldom got to discuss home and family. My problems were small compared to his, but they were important, too. After all, I tried to take an interest in his work. I would have taken more of an interest in it, except that one day I suggested something that might allow him to spend less time with the business and more with his family.

Renaud didn't like the idea, said so and laughed. I was indignant. "I resent being treated like a second-class moron," I said.

"You want to be treated like a first-class moron?" he asked, with a wicked gleam in his eyes.

Then there was a worse-than-usual day, with everything going wrong — until I opened the door for Renaud in the evening. There he stood, tired, dirty, with a stubble of beard, a shy grin and a big bouquet of golden yellow brown-eyed Susans that he'd jumped a fence to gather for me on the way home.

So the best discovery of all was that almost every frustration and disappointment had its compensations. Not always immediately, of course, and not always in tangible form. Sometimes just a flash of insight, an appreciation, a realization that there was value to hanging in there.

* * * * ○ * * * *

CHAPTER 24

Don't Just Sit There — Do Something

As the years passed and our family expanded, the country couldn't have done anything nicer for us than to provide summer neighbors.

The Campbells, Helen and Colin, were raising a family, too, and moved into their new summer cottage, five properties east of us, during the summer Billy was two years old.

Their children, Malcolm, Anne and Colin, Jr., plus our three, maintained a full summer schedule between the two households. Rain or shine, the six of them were busy all the time. So were we mothers.

The children made go-carts, log cabins in the woods, tree houses and a large raft, christened by the firm splat of a plastic bag of champagne (pink-tinted water) on the deck. This raft was so unstable that it tilted up and down like a seesaw, sending the children slipping and sliding from one end to the other, and so heavy that in a strong wind we could be sure it would break anchor and leave port, soon to be pursued by streams of shrieking children running out of the cottages and chasing down the shoreline.

They also got involved in business ventures to earn pocket money. One profitable project was clams. The clams in our bay are tough, inedible and prolific, and have no regard for the dozens of Campbell and Caza toes scampering through the waves.

After several summers of treating minor cuts and rushing one summer visitor to hospital for stitches from a clam shell gash, Helen and I decided it was time to wage war.

We offered the children one cent for every clam shell they brought in. It didn't take long to change our tune to one cent for two, and eventually, to slow them down and get out of a hopeless glut on the market, a cent for five shells. Word traveled fast, and the harvesters from far and near brought clams by the hundreds, not just from in front of our properties either, depositing them in green plastic garbage bags, counting off the shells and presenting the bill.

I came to dread the slap, slap of bare feet against the concrete walk, accompanied by the clunk-chunk of bouncing bags of clam shells as an awful thought occurred to me: The swimming area was clear of clams now, but the real question was how the defunct clams would hold up in all this heat and humidity while waiting for the garbage collection, four days away. It didn't take four days to find out.

Another money-making scheme involved worms. Great, fat, juicy night crawlers sell to the local marina in lots of one thousand, and the boys were full of enthusiasm about getting a niche in that market.

The best time to go hunting night crawlers is, of course, at night, when they are crawling. So the boys would set the alarm clock for 1:00 A.M. get togged out in old, dark clothes so they wouldn't scare the worms, and skulk out into the night, crouched over, treading softly in a fine, light drizzle ("But Mom, that's the best time!").

They gathered their quota once, but the part that made me quiver was that they actually counted out the one thousand worms, exactly, before taking them to the marina. I was frankly relieved when this juvenile business venture bit the dust.

Linda, the youngest of the Caza trio, was no fisherman, but she was always a willing assistant when her brothers netted minnows to stock their private gallon-pickle-jar aquarium. When she was old enough to be recruited, Billy and Joey handed her a dipper of minnows in icy lake water and told her to run into the house and dump them into a basin of water. Linda, full of motherly sympathy for the fish, first filled the basin in the sink with warm water, because the minnows must be cold, dumped in the minnows and then, because they must be hungry, too, added a couple of handfuls of dry oatmeal. When Billy and Joey came running in for the dipper, the minnows were swimming in a sticky, porridgey gruel from which they were rescued, rinsed off gently and given their freedom without a second to spare.

When the children weren't clamming, worming, fishing or rafting, they were running. Rain or shine, nothing dampened their young spirits. In summer, the Caza and Campbell youngsters drilled an express trail across the lakeside properties between our place and theirs, often picking up from six to ten extra assorted shapes and sizes as they roared along past the newer cottages, preparing to descend en masse on one or another household, there to hold court for anywhere from half an hour to the entire afternoon.

Any mother in the middle of something demanding concentration, like hanging wallpaper or making a new maternity dress, knew it was time to put everything away until the invading troops had finished their current project or could be diverted elsewhere.

When they settled in for a long siege, Helen and I would carry our coffee down to the dock, next to the sand pile and watch them tunnel to China in the sand. Or if we were feeling particularly courageous, we would turn the house over to them while we got on with our sewing or cleaning, first making sure nothing important and edible was sitting in plain view in the kitchen. (This last safety measure was instituted after the time I left a freshly iced cake on the counter while I answered the telephone only to come back and find ten empty milk glasses and a few pathetic crumbs.)

Another time I returned from Helen's to find that my shoes stuck to the kitchen floor with each step — the direct result of the children spilling a two-quart container of Kool-Aid on the floor, swooshing the mop over it and departing with the virtuous feeling that they'd cleaned the floor for me and left it nice and shiny, too.

And there was the time another summer neighbor went back to her cottage to find that the combined forces of eight children (Helen's, mine and hers) had polished off an entire bottle of crème de menthe, which they'd mixed with sugar and water. They thought it was peppermint Kool-Aid — "Gee, Mom, that's what it tasted like . . ."

Then the boys discovered overnight camping in the wild.

The first time set the pace. Billy and Joey, who were then fourteen and twelve, respectively, ran into the kitchen one Tuesday in August, pausing only when close enough to open the refrigerator.

"Mom," they yelled.

"I'm here," I said.

"We're going camping."

Billy reached in the fridge for a wedge of leftover pizza; Joey reached for another. They slammed the door, ran to the table with pen and paper, and Bill wrote "Camping Supplies" at the top of the page.

"What?" I exclaimed.

"Camping, Mom."

"When?" I asked. "Next Summer?"

"This weekend," said Billy, bounding up from the table to get milk and glasses.

"Wait a minute," I said. "Have you thought this through carefully? Do you know anything at all about camping?"

"Sure, Mom. We learned all about it in Scouts," said Billy.

"Ah, yes, but where is there to go camping around here?" I asked. Not a good question, since we're surrounded on one side by cottages, one side by more or less wilderness and two sides by water.

"We thought we'd go down the LaGuerre River and camp a few miles back in the woods," said Billy. The LaGuerre is a narrow but navigable river flowing past the south side of our property and into the lake. They planned to follow it inland.

"Who would go with you?" I meant some responsible adult.

They meant: "Well, we thought with the two of us, and Malcolm and Colin, and Andy and Cousin Yves . . ."

"This weekend, huh?" I asked.

"Yeah. And wait'll you see the stuff we're bringing. Andy's got a neat knapsack, and we've all got sleeping bags — and there'll be Malcolm's pup-tent and mine," said Billy.

"Two tents?" I asked. "For six of you? Why, that won't be enough."

"Ah, don't worry, Mom. We'll all share."

"What if it rains?" I protested.

"Hey, Neat-O!"

"What about . . ."

"Mom — it's O.K.!"

But of course the boys knew how to camp. Hadn't they always returned safe — if somewhat in need of a good washing — from Scout camp? Of course they had.

Still, as the week progressed, I had a hard time reconciling their preparations with the way we got ready for Scout camp. The main difference was that now nobody was going to tell them what they could bring or what they had to eat. Especially beans.

They certainly weren't having anything to do with Sputnik Stew, one Scout leader's lethal last-night-at-camp supper effort of combining all the remaining goods, including peaches and peas, into a large pot, adding the rest of the ketchup and relish, and boiling briskly.

While our campers agreed on such basics as bacon, eggs and hot dogs, each wanted special personal favorites. Vast quantities of soft drinks, potato chips, popcorn, gum, chocolate bars, cookies, snack cakes, pretzels and nuts were jammed into pillow cases and pockets, destined to arrive at the camp site warm, crumbly and squishy.

The boys prepared well in advance. Because our house is on the banks of the LaGuerre River — across the road and over the bridge from the launch site, our family room sprouted an astonishing growth of dunnage bags, tents, water canteens, sleeping bags, mosquito repellent, shovels, flashlights, fishing equipment, comic books and transistor radios.

Camping day arrived. Early in the morning they carried the Campbell's aluminum boat across the road and over the bridge to the banks of the LaGuerre, lowered it into the river and attached a rubber supply dingy to the stern by two long tow ropes. Then they hauled the provisions across the road and over the bridge, passing everything bucket-brigade fashion from one to the other until enough lumpy bags of supplies bristled from the rubber dingy and the aluminum boat to put Santa's sleigh to shame.

The boys then settled wherever they could. One even perched unsteadily on top of the supplies — and shoved off for a few days of independence and adventure.

Mothers, sisters, dogs and passers-by stood on shore, and cars stopped on the bridge over the river to watch, cheer and wave off the campers as they waggled down the winding little river and out of sight beyond the bullrushes and dense brush, singing raucous camp songs at the top of their lungs.

The rest of the adventure belonged to them alone: choosing a campsite, unloading knapsacks, sleeping bags and frying pans, and trudging through the woods totally independent of parental ties and maternal concern. Then there was sleeping out under the stars; telling stories around the campfire; listening with fearful anticipation to the snap of a twig, the rustle of a dry branch, the hoot of an owl or the scurrying of little four-footed creatures through the underbrush. Camp evenings are thrilling; nights deliciously terrifying with the sounds of the forest, as tender heads are drawn deep within the warm protection of cosy sleeping bags.

Mornings are another story. Hungry boys start the fire and proceed to melt my Tupperware, bend my Teflon and scratch around in knapsacks for bacon, eggs, butter and even — ah, luxury — pancake mix and syrup.

There lies ahead a busy day of exploring, fishing, gathering wood for the fire, clearing up the campsite, shaking crumbs out of sleeping bags, making preparations for the next meal and digging holes for burying garbage, bacon grease and broken cups.

The time they forgot to take the grill to place over the fire and had nothing to support the frying pan, they cooked their meal by placing the pan on a grill Joey made by weaving springy willow twigs together. Just as the food began to smell wonderful to the famished campers, the twig grill burned through and pan and contents took a dive into the embers — gone forever.

When they forgot sugar for the cocoa, Joey separated

Oreo cookies and scraped the icing into the cups for sweetener. When I asked him later how it was, he didn't answer.

Every year there are misadventures, such as someone forgetting that the frying pan handle is hot and dumping the breakfast, or someone dropping the pot of cocoa on the fried eggs. Or someone falls on the carton of eggs or accidentally douses the fire with the soup. Everyone trips on roots, tears shirts on branches, and on the last camping trip, cousin Yves lost his sweater in the water and had to get it out with the paddle, soaking wet and now useless in the cold night air.

Someone always gets holes burned in his sleeping bag because of curling up too close to the embers, and they can always count on a tent, or the provisions lean-to, caving in.

One year they wasted a lot of time peeling the skins off sausages. "We thought it was plastic," said Billy.

"It sure looked like plastic," said Joey.

These trips are sometimes complicated further by the dangers of the wild. "A cow almost attacked us," Billy once reported. And, as Joey admitted, "We fall down a lot."

They have to get used to the discomforts of away-from-home. A mattress made of twigs and branches; a knapsack for a pillow, a bush and a hole in the ground for a bathroom; and no television. They also have to wash their own dishes, though I have my doubts about that, because when they come back tired and bruised but happy, there's not so much as a clean spoon in the knapsack. Everything is covered with grease and black soot, and the only boy to return clean is the one who falls in the river on the way home.

✳ ✳ ✳ ✳ ○ ✳ ✳ ✳ ✳

CHAPTER 25

In the Wet

"*I'm sick,*" David moaned.

"Me too," said Joey.

Joey's friend David had come to spend a month with us, and they were campaigning for a day off from school. Every morning they pleaded, "Take my temperature, take my temperature." At the end of the school day they oozed off the bus coughing and holding their heads tragically.

"Don't I have a fever?" David asked pleadingly.

"No, David," I said. "I'm sure you don't."

"I'm really sick, Mom," said Joey. "*Really* sick."

"You look healthy to me, Joey," I said.

Every day was the same. They looked down each other's throats, examined each other's ears, looked in the mirror, stuck out their tongues, rolled their eyes to see how bloodshot they were and said, "I think I'm getting a cold."

One day the school had a sports field day. Neither David nor Joey was involved in the events. Besides, Joey's leg was in a full cast, so being a mother, not a saint, I weakened and allowed them to stay home.

They had a wonderful day, wore sloppy sweatsuits, luxuriated in TV movies, home-made popcorn, hot chocolate and comic books.

At supper time I asked them if they'd enjoyed their day off.

"Fine," said Joey.

"Yeah, great," said David. "Gee, I'd never have been able to do this if I'd been home."

"What do you mean?" I asked. "You might have taken a sports day off. Why wouldn't you have been able to?"

"Because," said David, licking the ice cream from the top of a cone I'd just handed him, "my Dad's too smart for that. He'd never have let me get away with it."

I'd been had.

The first time Joey brought David to the house was for a weekend visit. It was a bad-weed time, and the lake near shore was a minor Sargasso sea of stringy masses of tangled weeds and grasses, dislodged by Seaway traffic out in the channel. These weedy masses, along with whatever dead marine life they ensnared, are pushed by winds and currents right into our bay, where they end up pressing against our shoreline. We don't like it, but we've learned to live with it.

The kids jumped off the school bus at five-thirty, surged hungrily into the house, threw their books in the corner and glued themselves around the kitchen table. I gave them supper while Billy told David about the great fishing, Joey introduced him to our dog and Linda told him that if he didn't like the meals we had Shredded Wheat.

After supper they did their homework and settled in the living room to watch TV while I had supper with Renaud, who got home around nine. Before bedtime, the boys and Linda decided to take David outside to show him around. David slipped into his red nylon jacket as he ran out the door, following Joey, Billy and Linda to the beach.

It was a beautiful evening, with a full autumn moon casting a golden shimmer on the dark lake. The children sauntered along the concrete walk edging the water, chatting with excitement about the fun they were going to have. Renaud and I stood in the doorway with our coffee, watching them and enjoying the happy chatter and late evening peace.

Suddenly, David, without a word, turned and sprang the foot or so from the concrete walkway to the flat surface below, but it wasn't there. He sank like a stone into three feet of dirty, stringy water, thick with weeds, went sprawling full length, then disappeared.

After flailing about for a few moments, regaining his balance and standing up, David looked around at his surroundings, down at his messy self and up at Billy, Joey and Linda, who had been standing stunned and motionless for the first few seconds, but who were now holding onto each other and roaring in unrestrained glee. David stood dripping, asking only, "Wha' happened?"

He waded to shore, climbed up on the grassy bank, and Billy, Joey and Linda, weak with laughter, followed him to the house.

With clothes hung on the clothesline, weeds picked out of his hair and from behind his ears, and shoes blotted dry with paper towels, David brought his first day in the country to a close with a flourish.

Living close to the water gave me many nervous moments. In the beginning, when they were very small, I worried about the children falling in and didn't trust them out of my sight. As they got older, bolder and faster, my concerns escalated. They loved the water. All their friends loved the water.

They bought snorkles, flippers and underwater gear. They roared out of the house, leaving piles of abandoned clothes festooned over the furniture and strewn on the floor, hurled themselves off the pier and churned out to the raft where they and their friends spent hours diving, laughing, pushing, shrieking, falling and working up vast appetites.

There was also the sport of throwing friends into the water, sometimes fully clothed, and sometimes with fingers still clutching the arms of aluminum lawn chairs.

This is not too bad when the water is clear, which is most of the summer, but we who do the laundry, mop floors, count noses, bandage toes and make endless peanut butter sandwiches and Kool-Aid, know that in August tons of weeds drift in to become an eyesore — and a smelly one. Throwing friends in the water (especially in August) is not a relaxing spectator sport. Still, over the years, I have tried to adjust to it.

I have now reached the stage where I can remain in my lawn chair, casually turning pages of unrealistic magazines describing the peace of country living, in spite of the *squelch*, *squish* sounds of the current throwee shuffling moistly past my lawn chair, dripping, weedy and often smelling to high heaven as he sloshes toward the clothesline to dispose of as many outer garments as modesty allows before tip-toeing through the house to rummage around for something dry.

In time I got used to the children's water sports, but Renaud, busy earning a living six days a week, was unprepared for the activity that erupted one Sunday afternoon.

"What are they *doing*?" he exclaimed in alarm as a surge of a dozen or so teenaged boys whooped and hurled themselves toward a bunch of teenaged sisters and neighbor girls arrested in mid-saunter as they emerged from the house with handfuls of cookies.

"Chasing the girls, from the looks of it," I answered mildly.

"What for?" Renaud asked apprehensively, half rising from his lawn chair as doors slammed, shrill howls and shrieks filled the air, and bodies lurched and flung past us as the pursued ran for shelter from the pursuers.

"Gonna throw them in the water, it seems," I said nonchalantly.

"But they're all dressed," Renaud protested.

"Huummmm," I said. "How about another cup of coffee?"

CHAPTER 26

* * * * ○ * * * *

Love Me, Love My Doggie

Household pets were always part of my growing years, but the furthest thing from my mind when we got married was whether or not we would have a dog.

Renaud grew up with animals around, too, though on the farm they were not part of the household, but part of the workforce. Cats caught mice and bunked in the hayloft; dogs rounded up the cows. Once, brother-in-law Maurice's dog even rounded up my friend Beth's beige Volkswagen when she was driving home from her teaching job and just happened to get in the way of the cows being brought to the milking barn across the road. The dog was a tenacious border collie and according to Beth it was either run him down, or follow him in.

In our own home the subject of pets didn't come up right away. We were busy. Time passed. Then suddenly, Renaud noticed that he had three pre-school kids running around the house, remembered how he loved his dog when he was young and turned his talents to searching out and bringing home dogs.

He was determined to add another dependent to the family. A dependent with four mud-attracting feet, poor timing and kitchen privileges. That's when I realized that I, who had been crazy about animals when someone else was looking out for them, was not nearly so thrilled when they were tacked onto my expanding list of responsibilities like an ungainly postscript.

Renaud didn't want to get involved in their care either, aside from instructing me. "Margie," he would say. "That dog is filthy. Why do you *let* him go down into the swamp?" and "Margie, did you see what your dog did to the neighbor's garbage?" Then, when I tried to do something about it: "Margie, we live in the country. You can't tie a dog up. That's what turns them vicious. Free. Let him run free!"

The children weren't much help either. Every stray dog that wandered down Highway 132 was fair prey to our animal-loving offspring. Even if obviously well cared for, sleek and chubby, with licence tag jingling prominently, they would look at it with longing. If it made the mistake of hesitating, the children said, "Oh, poor little lost doggie," and made a bee-line up the driveway to overwhelm the now-bewildered animal with promises of a good time. Then they'd lure him down to the house, get him a pan of water and chocolate chip cookies and give him a grand tour of the house and grounds.

Overcome by all this attention, the doggie stranger would wag and cavort around for hours, having fun, fun, fun with his new friends. Then he'd suddenly think about home, look startled, take stock of the situation and belatedly head for home.

Sometimes, however, the whole thing would be too much, and the confused mutt would settle in, leaving me to track down his owner by his licence tag number, with sometimes a long distance call or two.

The children were pushovers for livestock. Over the years our household has played host to birds, rabbits, turtles, hamsters, white mice, praying mantises, fish, two invalid seagulls, a sick duck named Molly and a bright-eyed but unambitious pony named Charlie that a customer had sold to Renaud. We bought a sulky and entered Charlie in the pony races in Ste. Barbe, and we'd all go down to the track on Sunday afternoons and yell, "Come on, Charlie," in spite of the fact that after the first lap around the track Charlie always ran out the gate and back to the stable.

Much as I tried to discourage Renaud from adding dogs to the household, I didn't always take my own advice. Like that hot mid-summer morning when a defeated, beaten-looking dog, almost as big as a pony, stumbled aimlessly down the road in front of our house, pausing every few steps on the searing pavement. He stopped to look longingly toward us. Who could resist?

We brought him a pan of water, coaxed him down the driveway, and he moved in. He was the biggest German Shepherd I had ever seen. He had tremendous, quiet dignity, and it was clear that under the rags and tatters of his shabby black and cream coat he was a magnificent animal.

From the time he came, Rex never left our property unless accompanied by one of the family. When outside alone, he attached himself to the house like a barnacle. He wouldn't stay alone in the house either. The few times I left him there and went out, he dived through screened windows.

I couldn't even run over to Helen's for coffee anymore, because Rex and their beagle, Ami, didn't see eye-to-eye. After one suspense-filled coffee-break, Helen and I decided that it would be safer in future not to invite a real knock-down-drag-out between such unequal opponents and decided that, from then on, our coffee breaks should be held at my house.

But one day I tried to outwit Rex. I set a dish of food outside near the back door. While he was busy with that, I raced through the house, out the front door, across the property and out of sight behind the cedar hedges, leaving Rex to think I was still in the house. The plan worked beautifully. When I returned, there was Rex, leaning up against the back door, guarding the house quite contentedly — but obviously surprised to see me come across the lawn.

I was delighted that the ruse had been so successful. The next day I went through the same preliminaries. His lunch dish full and set outside at the same place, I ran through the house, out the front door, onto the driveway and came face to face with Rex. He had picked up his dish in his teeth and carried it to the middle of the driveway where he could command a good view of front and back.

We were sorry when we found Rex's owner two months later, who said that Rex had disappeared when out for his nightly run six months earlier and eighty miles away. He'd probably been stolen and then escaped. The happy reunion was all we needed to persuade us to let him go.

Soon after Rex left, Renaud came home with a look of jubilation on his face, stood in the living-room doorway and said, "Guess what!"

"A dog," yelled Joey. "You've brought us a dog!" Immediately all three children headed toward the door.

"Wait a minute," Renaud cautioned, blocking the doorway. And he began to prepare us for the unattractiveness of the unfortunate animal he had just bought from a farmer who was going to have him destroyed. But of course, anyone with children knows that a peculiar fact about animal-loving kids is that the worse the condition of the animal, the more intense is the love generated.

"I just couldn't leave him there," explained Renaud as he brought the neglected little beast into the house.

The dog was a pitiful sight, with a thin, soiled, smelly yellow coat that barely stretched over protruding bumps of angular bone.

"Oh, Mom," enthused Joey, "He's beautiful!"

"What'll we call him?" "Does he have a name?" "How old is he?" The usual questions. They brought him a bowl of milk and a few table scraps, which he ate greedily. The next morning I drove him to the vet. "The works," I said as the small skinful of dirty fur cringed on the examining table. (I hadn't dared wash him. He was much too frail to survive contact with water.)

"I'll give him a worm capsule and some other medication," said the vet as he checked the dog.

"How about a rabies shot?" I asked. The doctor said the dog was so far gone from malnutrition that a rabies shot would be too much for him.

While I drove along the highway on the way home, the dog became active at both ends all over the back seat. Ah well, every family should have a dog.

"Scooter," as we called him, became a member of the family. Of uncertain breed, he grew long and lanky with sort of a collie look. It was his habit to wait until everyone was out of the house and sneak into our bedroom to curl up on our bed. He thought he had us fooled because we never actually caught him at it, but we were always aware of the warm, round depression at the foot of the bed.

Scooter was usually careful to take his sleeping-on-the-bed nap when nobody was home, but one Sunday morning he got careless.

It was Father's Day. Billy had a speech to recite at mid-point of each of the four masses at St. Anicet's church. For the first one Billy and I got up quietly, dressed and left without disturbing the household. I heard afterward what had happened.

Apparently, when the door clicked shut, Scooter woke up, ran to the kitchen window, saw the car leaving and thought Renaud and I were in it. Loping eagerly into our bedroom, he vaulted his lanky frame into the air, and with the velocity of a buzz-bomb crashed down onto Renaud's stomach, whereupon both man and beast surged into the air, bellowing in outrage and surprise.

Renaud's surprise definitely had the edge, because having thirty-five-odd pounds of squirming bone, fur and muscle suddenly descend on a relaxed abdomen is not the best start in the world to a peaceful Sunday.

Scooter didn't stay around to argue with the disgruntled master of the house, but quickly slithered off the bed, shot across the room and disappeared around the corner, not to be seen for the rest of the morning.

CHAPTER 27

* * * * ○ * * * *

Happy

For a while we had a transient Red Setter named Ruby, who
entered through doors, exited through windows, gave us an
open account with the glaziers and, for the first time, fleas.
Then one day Ruby packed her bags and walked out. We
heard that she'd moved in with another family a few miles
away and that she still preferred windows to doors.

Nobody ever "owned" Ruby. She was a gypsy at heart and
kept changing residences, until one day Renaud called on a
customer whose wife's name was Ruby, and there, sure
enough, was "*our*" Ruby. She probably heard the farmer call
his wife one day, thought he meant her, and moved in. At last
count, she was still there.

One of our favorite dogs was a con artist Renaud brought
home one day when we had been dogless for almost four
months. The dog bounded into the house, wagged his way to
the children and frisked around in a boisterous way, laughing, chuckling and even smiling.

"Look how happy that dog is!" exclaimed Joey. And
"Happy" it's been ever since.

Happy is black, with rust-rimmed ears, rust mock-eye-
brows and a white blaze on his chest. In winter he grows
thick fur clumps under his paws, like fur slippers squirting
up between his toes.

156

In repose, he lies on his bony spine, legs and forearms in the air and spraddled out, and neck stretched to show off his sleek russet throat.

Happy has no objection to the bread man coming to the door, but is suspicious of the milkman and absolutely detests the garbagemen.

At night he sneaks into Renaud's chair as soon as Renaud goes to bed. When Renaud starts out the door in the morning, the dog crawls into the chair again, taking sly sidelong glances to see if anyone is going to object.

Happy can't talk, of course, but he does say, "Hello." It comes out as a resonant "HeeRROOooooo." When Renaud comes home for dinner, he offers dog biscuits to Happy, getting a good "HeeRROOOoooo" for each one. And he joins in with the singing when the children have a musical jam session.

Happy sits like a person. When the children leave for school in the morning, or when he thinks it's time for them to come home in the afternoon, he sits in the stairway by the kitchen window facing north — the direction of the school bus. Standing on the first step, he turns around and backs his seat onto the second step, feet dangling over the edge, and leans his arms on the windowsill with his chin resting on his paws.

In fact, he's never learned to sit like a dog. Even when sitting on the floor he has the same problem. He doesn't sit on his haunches, but right on his bony bottom, with his feet sticking straight out in front, which makes him slide backward or tip over, so he has to concentrate if he intends to sit for any length of time.

Happy is also playful. If I decide on a sunny morning that I want to whiten the sheets and pillow cases as Grandma used to by spreading them on the grass in full sun, I go out fifteen minutes later to find them hauled halfway across the yard or lying there with a trail of muddy dog-prints stamped across them.

Happy's favorite spot is under the furniture. When he was younger and smaller, he used to crawl under the bed, under the living-room chairs and under the footstool. Gradually, it became apparent to everyone but Happy that he didn't fit anymore. Unwilling to accept that he was no longer a puppy, he would struggle, squirm and complain until he was firmly stuck between spring and floor. Realizing his predicament, he would then claw frantically at the floor to gain traction, and would eventually have to be rescued.

As with most dogs who live in the house with their adoptive families, Happy became less a pet and more one of the kids. The usual promises made beforehand that Mother will never have to feed the dog, clean and fill his water dish, mop up puddles, wipe mud off his paws, comb burrs out of his fur or do any other dog-related chores, are easily forgotten. After all, who's at home all day when the children are at school and Happy cavorts across the road and into a field full of burdocks with his Labrador friend Boots? Who but Mother knows the complicated technique required for lifting and disposing of the impressive and smelly contents of his stomach when he's thrown up under the kitchen table just when everyone else has started on their bacon and eggs?

The Campbells were as much victim to livestock bought for the kids' sake as we were. They had, besides Ami, a black and white cat named Francis, a gerbil named Rusty and a large box turtle by the name of Samantha. Samantha had the run of the house, and the spectator sport of the Samantha era was watching disbelieving guests react to Samantha sauntering through the living room and down the hallway.

The Campbells also had two parakeets known as Herbie and Julie. Herbie, a tough, determinedly social old bird, was disappointed in Julie's quiet nature. His unsympathetic attitude caused his eviction to another cage one day when Helen found Julie huddled in terror on the floor of the cage and Herbie, with all the sensitivities of a pirate, standing over her, complaining loudly and kicking her.

But of all the livestock in the Campbell home, Ami is king.

He is a chubby, solid little beagle, white, tan and black, with expressive brown eyes, a loose frown, velvet ears and a possessive attitude toward anything remotely edible. This last trait did not bring out the best in Happy, who could walk past a bone dozens of times without batting an eye, but had only to see Ami heading for the same bone to lay claim to it himself — as a point of honor.

It got so that Happy would even drop a bone in plain sight, hide behind a tree, then peer with mock unconcern at the treasure, waiting for Ami (sporting, as he sometimes does, a Dole banana sticker in the middle of his forehead) to come loping along and spot the bone. And the battle would be on.

Summers bring added risk because the children run the trail between the cottages, dribbling an excess of potato chips and popcorn, thus precipitating frequent free-for-alls, with the dogs breaking through hedges, falling off piers and engaging in furious battles, complete with swirling dust, sand and fur. With teeth showing viciously below curled lip, and growls and yips of pain and rage, they scream and swear at each other as the whole neighborhood gathers around, encouraging them on to greater efforts or pleading tearfully with them to stop.

When they are finally separated, with the aid of buckets of cold water, lawn chairs and rakes wedged between them, they are dragged home in disgrace. Later the fight is recounted blow-by-blow as the children argue about who started the fight, who drew blood, who inflicted the most damage, who was the victor and who the vanquished.

When the Campbell's daughter, Anne, returned from dragging Ami home after the last big dog fight — during which Billy got a bite on his wrist and was thoroughly drenched when Malcolm missed with the bucket of water — she said that as she pushed Ami over the threshold, he was clasping his paws over his head triumphantly in a self-declared gesture of championship.

Actually, the dogs are friends most of the time. But Happy is faster on his feet than his short-legged beagle friend and often lures him into a chase. At such times, Helen and I, along with the children and all the neighbors, stop everything, move out of the way and watch the show as the two dogs steam along full tilt in ever-widening circles, falling into the lake, barging through flower beds, hedges and picnic tables, and occasionally ramming into tree trunks, oblivious to everything but the glorious chase.

Happy runs and Ami chases, but the wily Ami soon developed a countertactic of doubling back, crouching behind a bush or tree, and pouncing at Happy as he galloped past, whereupon they would both explode into the air and flail about in a windmill of snarling teeth and gripping claws until they let go and the chase was on again.

In summer, Happy chases the waves as they chop and hit against the shore. He leaps through the water, yelping gleefully as he bounds into the air like an antelope, carving graceful arcs with each leap, choking on huge gulps of the whitecaps, and being knocked flat by the more strenuous waves. He can keep this up by the hour, or for as long as he has an audience, or until his knees buckle from fatigue.

Happy thinks of himself as a superb watchdog. When neighbors tip-toe innocently across our property in the dead of night to get to their own cottage, he lets go with some of the most blood-curdling yodelling imaginable, yanking the entire household bolt upright in terror. On the other hand,

I've often wondered what might be accomplished by a clever thief with a dog biscuit.

Happy's self-styled home-protection service was put to the test recently when a truck pulled up in the driveway and five men came into the back yard to remove the snow fences. Screaming in outrage, Happy raced through the house and flung himself bodily against the back door. The door unexpectedly flew open and he tumbled out, right at the feet of the astonished workers.

It was a much humbler Happy who turned tail, scrunched low to the ground and crawled over the step into the protection of the house to the accompaniment of loud guffaws of laughter from the workmen.

Happy also likes to think of himself as a brave hunter, though I have seen him thoroughly intimidated by a neighbor's kitten. He does, however, wander up and down the highway, along the waterfront and through the fields, bringing home every dead body within a radius of half a mile, depositing the sometimes skeletal and decaying remains on the front step and banging his paws urgently against the door, so we will come and see just what a great hunter he is and what a grand prize he's brought home.

I suppose the reason we've never been able to discourage him from this disgusting pastime is that the children greet his sudden gifts with hysterical screams and shrieks, perhaps interpreted by him as indications of delight. Then one of us (guess who) rushes out with a shovel or piece of cardboard and scoops up the ghastly remains, depositing them as quickly as possible into a plastic garbage bag.

Perhaps he thinks we're saving them to stuff or frame.

I'll always remember the day Happy brought home one of his smellier trophies. It was late summer, and the weeds near shore were thick. In the midst of all this vegetation, Happy had joyously discovered a very large, very dead, very rotten eel, floating white and belly-up.

Immensely impressed with his prowess, he waded in, grabbed his inert quarry, struggled ferociously with it, just long enough for it to fall to pieces around and over him, and dragged home the disgusting remains. He was looking for congratulations.

He didn't get them. As soon as we had pulled ourselves together, we got armed for battle. A bottle of detergent, a bar of soap, a bottle of shampoo and, to finish things off, a bottle of creme rinse. We then lured him off the end of the concrete walkway next door where the water was clean. Then the children took over and towed him out to deep water.

Happy, who normally loves water to an insane degree, immediately became convinced that we were trying to dissolve him in acid and started whimpering, shivering and trembling as soon as he saw the bar of soap — which was not logical, since he is forever gnawing at the cake of Ivory resting on the edge of the bathtub.

The children lathered and rinsed him, lathered and rinsed him again, and then started all over again. Finally, they applied the creme rinse and dragged him to deeper water for a brisk swim.

Gaining his freedom, Happy escaped in flying leaps, plunging toward shore, there to plow once more through the smelly part of the shoreline and up onto the beach.

The children churned out of the water, tackled him and carried him back into the water to go through another wash and rinse cycle.

This time they hung on and carried him via the clean route, back to shore, wrapped him in blankets and towels in the sunshine and rubbed him dry.

Joey ran into the house, returning with a bottle of perfume, and dumped the entire contents over him.

For days we knew Happy was around without even seeing him. Whenever he sauntered up behind the neighbors, they turned around expecting to greet a perfumed lady visitor, only to find a black dog with red eyebrows and bright smiling eyes, blissfully unaware that he did not live up to his calling card.

CHAPTER 28

* * * * * ○ * * * *

Don't Sit on the Cat

It was early spring as Renaud drove me home from the hospital, where I'd just had minor surgery. I was lulled by his cheerful chatter and the warmth of the sunlight streaming through the car window. Renaud was obviously delighted that we were getting back to normal, and told me how smoothly things were running, how the children shared the housework, how the business was doing all right. Everything I wanted to hear.

Still, he seemed preoccupied. A few miles before the house he slowed the car and the conversation, cleared his throat and introduced a new topic.

"By the way," he said, laughing lightly, "there's a cat that comes around to the house."

"Oh?" I said.

"Yes," he replied. "It comes to the back door and cries, then to the front door, then climbs up on the windowsill, looks into the living room and cries."

Well, I've always liked cats, but Renaud never wanted one, so there didn't seem much for me to say at this point, so I said, "Really?"

Renaud said, "Yes, poor thing," adding, "Of course we haven't let it in the house."

"Of course," I said.

"I warned the children not to let it in," Renaud said.

"Uh hum," I agreed, nodding.

"And you shouldn't let it in the house either," he said, looking sidewise at me.

"I won't," I said.

"It's a beautiful cat . . ."

"Really?"

"Yes, the most beautiful cat I've ever seen."

"Hummm, is that so?"

"Yes. But it's very thin." He glanced over at me again. "We can't feed it you know," he said. "Someone must own it — such a beautiful cat."

"I understand," I said.

"If we feed it," said Renaud, "you know that we'll never get rid of it. And after all, our house is small. We already have a dog — we certainly don't need a cat, too."

All this I knew, but I began to have an uneasy feeling that "He doth protest too much."

The feeling deepened when we arrived at the house. Right there, beside the back door, sat a comfy cardboard box containing an old red wool sweater, a dish of milk, slightly frozen, and a dish of dog food. Since Happy is a big, lazy house dog, I felt reasonably sure that this little nest wasn't his.

Renaud managed to look surprised and said, "I'll bet the kids have been feeding that cat. I told them not to."

While his voice lacked the ring of conviction, I didn't want to be too hasty in my conclusions. I nodded. "I'll bet they have," I said quietly.

We went into the house and, while enjoying a cup of coffee and renewed togetherness, the school bus arrived with the children, who hurried in with hugs, kisses and chatter.

Suddenly a cat jumped up on the living room windowsill,

peered in and yowled. Renaud smiled blandly, leaped to this feet, kissed me goodbye, shot out the back door, got in the car and went back to work.

The "beautiful cat" was thin as a rake, black as a coal bin and had a yowl that made the hair on the back of my neck stand up.

Joey said we'd better let her in. Billy opened the door before I could protest, and Linda ran for the milk bottle and Happy's Alpo.

The children didn't seem at all confused or uncertain. Neither did the cat. Nor did Happy, who knew exactly what he wanted to do and proceeded to do it. Tooth and nail.

After we got the animals separated, I celebrated my first half-hour home with my loving family by yelling at the dog, yelling at the cat, yelling at the kids and wishing Renaud were there so I could yell at him.

When things calmed down, I learned that the cat had, of course, moved in, bag and baggage. In fact, the children said, it was Daddy — the same man who'd insisted that the last thing we needed was a cat in the house — who issued the invitation.

Renaud had the grace to look contrite when he came home for supper, though he smiled abashedly, too, as though he had done his good deed for the day and really, it was nothing — nothing at all. I didn't have to thank him.

The kids named the cat Putt-Putt, after a toy train commercial. We bought a catnip mouse, which Happy destroyed, and we bought cat kibble and put Putt-Putt's dishes on top of the refrigerator so the dog wouldn't get at them, though she steals from his dishes on the floor at will.

Putt-Putt was a serious, hot-headed creature with a mind of her own and no sense of humor. She was glad to be in from the cold and harbored a proprietary attitude toward settling on anything warmed by human flesh — recently vacated beds, hats, chairs or coats. It was dangerous, both for her and for us. After a few close calls, we learned to check first, sit later: it wasn't quite certain who would survive as a result of careless or hasty sitting, and nobody was eager to become a test case.

Happy and Putt-Putt knew they wanted to beat each other's brains out, but they tolerated each other eventually, even going so far as to play hide-and-seek. Putt-Putt hid around the corner, Happy stuck his head into the hallway and Putt-Putt zapped his nose, then arched her back, hissed fiercely and jumped up and down stiff-legged while Happy whined.

After a few weeks of this, Happy was so eager to sign a truce that he was pathetic. He sat, tail wagging uncertainly, head questioningly tipped to one side, strips of peeled skin dangling from his abused nose. Putt-Putt was in control.

Also in residence when Putt-Putt showed up was a hamster named Pinkey, who delighted the children by packing and unpacking his cheek pouches with sunflower seeds and just about anything else. Pinkey was especially fond of peanut butter and made a spectacle of himself by grabbing gobs of it in his fragile pink claws and stuffing it into his fat cheeks. Watching him unload this cargo was just as disgusting as the loading — if not worse, and Pinkey certainly didn't mind an audience.

We changed the debris in Pinkey's cage every day, for he was a prodigious worker and never happier than when in the midst of fresh cedar shavings and sheets of paper towelling. He outdid himself, though, the night I accidentally left a roll of paper towels just outside his cage. In the morning we couldn't see Pinkey, but there were strips and tufts of paper hanging from between the cage bars to the floor; the cage itself was stuffed to the top, and though he couldn't be seen, we could hear Pinkey shredding away industriously, content with his occupation.

Pinkey lived an unusually long and busy life. Perhaps because he always minded his own business, both Happy and Putt-Putt refused to acknowledge his presence in the house by so much as a woof or a hiss. And that was a lucky break, because I was having enough trouble controlling the menagerie without another territorial skirmish. I'm not really complaining, because I love animals, but look, I've done a lot of adjusting since becoming a wife and mother. I've adjusted to a husband who's smarter than I, a house that's smarter than both of us, a business that always gets its own way and three children with conflicting personalities (mostly conflicting with mine).

I've learned to live with a dog who smiles and says "Herrrooooo" before attacking, two love-doves who bill and coo loudly at sunrise, a hamster who sleeps all day and clanks around on his wheel all night (and no matter how much we oil it so it won't squeak, we can still hear it *woooosh* and *clank* quite clearly) and now I have to stand back for a cat who charges into the kitchen and flings herself possessively around every can being opened, and who perches on high furniture to attack anyone within cat-arm reach. Enough is enough. I'm telling you right now, nobody better bring home a canary!

CHAPTER 29

* * * * ○ * * * *

Winter

Mornings are not at their best in winter. Neither am I. Winter mornings are dark and cold. Between the cat, dog, children and Renaud I would far rather stay in bed than take part in the bedlam created by this assorted household struggling to its feet.

But it just isn't in me to lie there listening passively to ominous shrieks, piercing screams, crashes, slaps, hissed threats and, occasionally, an awe-filled "Uh-oh . . . look what the dog did under the table!" I usually manage to rise to the occasion and keep things moving in the direction of school bus and car. However, this is rarely accomplished calmly and with good grace.

Take one average January day, memorable only because it so typifies all the other weekday mornings of winter. Wrapped in my blue flannel robe, feet in shaggy pink slippers with black button eyes and whiskers (a Christmas gift from my mother), I sounded reveille in the boys' room. Billy, still burrowed in a nest of quilts, eyes shut, mumbled hopefully, "Are the roads icy?"

Joey's voice from the other bunk croaked, "Is it snowing?"

I told them the roads were clear. There would be school.

Happy bounded into the room and rocketed from one bunk to the other, coaxing them awake with cold, wet nose prodding sleepy, warm necks.

Joey rubbed his eyes, hugged the dog and said he'd dreamed all night and was very tired.

Billy grumbled, "You think *you're* tired!"

I went back to the kitchen, called up the stairway to Linda, pushed the cat out the door and put the coffee pot on the stove.

Billy groped his way to the stereo in the living room, put on what he calls music (I call noise), turned it up too loud and stumbled back to the bedroom to get dressed.

I turned the stereo down. Linda wandered into the kitchen, fully dressed. It always amazes me that Linda can be so awake so fast, hair brushed, shirt and tunic neat, stockings smooth and clean, shoes on the right feet.

Suddenly Billy exploded into the kitchen, holding up his rumpled school clothes. He'd forgotten to hang them up the night before. Ditto Joey. They would have to wear them anyway. If you think I'm going to haul out the ironing board at six-thirty in the morning . . .

I set the table, let the cat in, bagged Linda's school lunch, put jam, peanut butter and corn flakes on the table, plugged in the toaster and asked them what they wanted for breakfast.

"Egg," Joey called out.

"Waffles," said Billy.

"Toast," said Linda, "with cinnamon."

I put a frozen waffle in the toaster, an egg in the frying pan, maple syrup and ketchup on the table.

I set Joey's egg in front of him, passed toast and cinnamon to Linda, passed a waffle to Billy and put another into the toaster.

Joey, in a typical school-morning daze, elbow on the table, chin on fist, reached for the bottle of slow-moving ketchup and upended it over the egg, waking with a jolt and yelp when he discovered he had upended the wrong bottle and thin, sticky, expensive maple syrup was cascading over the dish, egg, table and his lap.

While Billy and Linda laughed uproaringly, I yelled. Joey

left to get cleaned up. I wiped up the mess, tried to rinse the syrup off the egg, gave up and cooked another.

I poured three glasses of milk. Linda reached for her toast, knocked her glass of milk over, and I sprang into action with mop and sponges, complaining loudly about careless children not watching what they're doing as I worked at the eight fluid ounces that looked like much more. Joey, returning in his Sunday slacks, took all this in and announced with a flourish, "O.K., fellows, here it comes . . ." Billy picked it up with "There's Lake Superior, and Lake Erie." As the flow cascaded over the edge of the table, the boys chorused in unison, "And *here* it *is* ladies and gentlemen — *Niagara Falls!*"

Renaud, whom I'd forgotten to call, just because I forgot — and how did that get to be *my* job anyway — leaped out of bed at that moment, practically launching himself into orbit, and catapulted into the kitchen, where he stood in his long thermal-knits, wild-eyed, outraged and rumpled.

"What's going on here?" he bellowed. "What time is it? Why didn't you call me? What's all the racket about?"

I answered: "World War III; quarter to seven; I forgot," and, "Racket? What racket?"

I glared at him briefly, poured another glass of milk for Linda, and as I returned the gallon jug to the refrigerator too quickly, banged it against the door. The whole thing dropped to the floor, shattering the jug and scattering chunks of jagged glass like small icebergs in the milky white sea that shot upward in surprise and then settled in unrestrained puddles and streams hurrying to the sanctuary of under the refrigerator and under the china cupboard.

Three young voices from around the table said, in close harmony, "OOOOOoooooo . . ."

Renaud shook his head, groaned and headed for the bathroom. I shut my eyes and gritted my teeth. There was no time for me to retreat to a nice quiet bathroom.

Three pairs of eyes followed me with interest. While I got out the mop again I heard a titter, then a giggle from the audience. A hushed voice said, "Wow, did you see that flood?" and as a lump rose in my throat I wondered if I couldn't be precariously close to hysteria. Probably . . .

However, with little time for either tears or laughter, I cleaned up the mess, picked up the broken glass and looked reproachfully at the three musketeers happily watching the floor show and not even trying to look sympathetic as they munched their breakfasts.

A few minutes later, after stowing the mop for the second time, I found a puddle on the floor of the family room. Happy! My fault really. I had been very tired the night before and hadn't let him out for his usual evening run. Which, if you want to be generous, you could say was his fault. Sometimes he goes out and returns in five minutes. Sometimes he's gone for two hours. I didn't feel like waiting if it happened to be his night for far-flung philandering.

Pressing the mop back into action I fumed at the dog, who couldn't have cared less, but did an impressive job of pretending to be sorry, flattening his chin on the floor, tucking his nose into his paws and looking up at me sweetly through remorseful eyes.

The children thought it was a great joke. They would! They had to catch the school bus, so there was no time for them to clean up the mess. Billy said that he guessed Happy considered the leg of the pool table the next best thing to a tree. I wondered if he would have been as cheerful if Happy had mistaken his guitar for a tree. I stalked across the kitchen and set the mop and the dog outside the back door.

Almost time for the school bus and time for final inventory. "Do you have your handkerchiefs? Your milk money, Linda? Your lunch money, boys? Did you brush your hair? Are your socks clean? Do you have your gym costume? Your mittens? *Pull that hat down over your ears!*"

Just then Renaud sailed calmly out of the bathroom, looking smooth and neat, surveyed the confusion with the raised eyebrows of one who could have done much better and said, "The school bus is here." The children rushed out into the crisp, cold morning, giving their parents pecks on the cheek. I shut the door. We had survived another bout of early morningitis. Or no, not yet. The door burst open, and Billy and Joey tore back in. They'd forgotten to put their boots on. The bus was waiting.

"Don't get nervous. Don't get nervous. Calm down," scolded Renaud, cool as could be, but contributing little, aside from aggravation, to the situation as the boys scrambled for their boots and slammed out the door again. Hurry, hurry! Quick, quick! See Billy run! See Joey run! See Mother run! Run, Mother, run! Sigh . . .

That's what weekdays are like. Weekends are something else. In winter we have no neighbors. The Campbells are back in the city and everything is dull, dull, dull. We love the country, and there's no doubt that it looks beautiful, even in winter. But it's lonesome — especially for the children.

"Let's play hide-and-seek," they might suggest. Though original hiding places are rare in our small house, the children are resourceful. When Joey hid between the spring and mattress of the bed in the master bedroom, Billy and Linda discovered where he was by the raised lumpiness, but took delight in pretending ignorance as they sat thoughtfully on the bed, wondering aloud where he could be. Joey, convinced they didn't know where he was, suffered in his self-inflicted prison until one giggle too many gave the plot away and he emerged beet red with the grid-work pattern of the wire bedsprings imprinted on his face.

Linda thought an empty green garbage bag in a corner of the kitchen would make a good hiding place. She stepped into it, drew it up, put a paper bag over her head and curled up on the floor in a corner of the kitchen. But Joey caught on right away. As he said when he saw the soft green plastic clinging in unlikely contours, "We don't have any garbage shaped like that!"

But this is dull stuff and what the children really want is visitors. Something to do and somebody besides family to do it with.

"We never do anything any more," they sulk.

"Nobody ever comes to see us," they complain.

"This winter will never end, and summer will never come," they wail, leaving the distinct impression that they've been imprisoned on The Rock without human contact for at least half their lives.

Certainly when there's a knock on the door in winter it's a signal for all hell to break loose.

The children wouldn't think of getting up quietly and walking to the door, preferring to bolt out of their chairs, race to the windows to see who's car is outside and run wildly back and forth cheering, shouting and colliding, accompanied by frantic barkings and scramblings from the dog.

Should it be a customer to see Renaud on business or any other mere adult, unaccompanied by small fry, Renaud and I apologize for the racket as the children slink back bitterly to their sad occupations, muttering, "How come nobody comes to visit *us*?" Sometimes they add, "Can I ask David out to spend the rest of the winter? He's always getting into such neat messes."

It was just such a dull winter Sunday when our friends Dorothy and Jules came with their sons Richard and Roger. Within minutes the house became a damp, cosy hive of activity as puddles of water formed around the boot pile in the living room. The household went from sullen silence to happy chaos as the children chattered and whooped and laid their plans for the day. After twenty minutes of bringing each

174

other up to date, they pulled on their boots and coats and rushed out into the cold with Happy to explore the thickness of the lake ice, the packability of the snow, the depth of the drifts, and to see how soaked they could get before coming back in.

As I put the kettle on for coffee, Renaud and Jules escaped to the local hang-out for a couple of beers and respite from the human storm. Dorothy mopped puddles off the floor in the living room while telling me about their new cat, Muffie, who recently decided that early morning entertainment was in order. Captivated by the sight of eyelashes, she parked herself on the bed directly in front of her chosen victim and watched intently until the first flutter or twitch of eyelash, then sprang to attack.

Dorothy made me feel I was not alone in the child-adult comprehension battle as she told me about her latest encounter with a nephew who'd occupied himself in the kitchen storage cupboards one day while she was on the phone by removing, and presenting to her with a proud flourish, all the labels from the canned goods. "Now we have to judge what we're having for supper on the basis of prices stamped on the cans and how they sound when they're shaken," Dorothy said wryly, setting the mop outside the door.

By the time the men breezed back in, Richard, Roger, Billy, Joey and Linda, accompanied by cousins Sylvie and Yves, surged into the living room with slushy snow clinging to their clothes. They tossed boots into the boot corner, hung up their coats, revved up the record player and settled around the kitchen table for sandwiches, cookies and hot chocolate.

Then it was game time, and time for decisions. Though Billy, Joey and Linda have to be content with each other as partners when we're alone (they don't have a choice), the minute there are visitors it's another story.

They play casino, blackjack, cheat, spit and crazy eights.

They play Monopoly, Probe, Careers, Green Ghost, Scrabble, Clue, Sorry, charades, Stockticker, Risk and anything else that's current and novel or old hat and fun. But nobody wants a brother or sister for a partner, including the visitors.

"I want Richard for my partner."

"And I want Roger."

"Aw, No. Then I'd have to take Billy and that's not fair. He's my brother."

"O.K., O.K., but if Yves gets Roger, then who'll have Billy?"

"Well if Linda has Sylvie, can't Yves and Richard play together?"

"Then what about *me*?"

"Let's draw straws!"

"Aw, that never works. I think Billy and Roger should play against Yves and Sylvie."

"No fair! She's my sister!"

Eventually, decisions are made and the games played, to the accompaniment of whoops of victory and wails of defeat. "It's your fault we lost. Why did you play that Jack on the King?"

"It was all I had."

"You cheated!"

"I did not."

"You did too!"

In the play-offs, the finalists were pitted against each other, while the rooting section roared around the table screaming encouragement at their favorites and flinging accusations and advice. Meanwhile, Dorothy, Jules, Renaud and I tried to have a serious discussion about current events, somewhat hampered by the occasional flying mitten and piercing shriek.

In the midst of all this, Happy skulked about near the door, which was suspicious because he generally likes to be right in the action. But we're wise to him, and an inspection revealed that his jaws were tightly closed and his cheeks were bulging somewhat on one side. A smuggler if there ever was one — and a guilty-looking one at that.

The children massed together and cornered him, prying his lips up over his teeth to reveal that snuggled in among the incisors was a brand-new, still-wrapped package of chocolate-pecan Turtles he'd found under Joey's pillow. There was a howl as the boys leaped to the rescue.

Games and excitement over for the moment, the children put on their coats and boots again and headed outdoors to take a look at the fishing shacks on the ice and see what was being caught. These shacks, strewn about on the ice of the bay about a quarter-mile out from shore, are grouped in little bunches, like a toy village. Also scattered at intervals, some closer to shore, are small fishing holes cut through the ice and marked with long branches or flags. Every hour or so, fishermen leave their heated shacks to make the rounds of these fishing holes, checking the bait and pulling in an occasional fish.

The kids poked along aimlessly. Then Roger, unfamiliar with the idea of the exposed fishing holes, ran on ahead. He didn't fall into a hole, but he did find one with a cedar branch sticking out as a marker.

Thinking it must be a danger marker, Roger set to work filling the hole with chunks of snow. Intent on his life-saving task, he looked up in surprise as the fisherman, to whom it belonged, ran toward him, yelling and cursing at this vandalism. Roger lost no time arguing, but turned and hot-footed it back to the house as fast as he could go while his friends, watching from closer to shore, laughed and cheered him on, until the fisherman's wrath turned on them, too, and they also found it wise to retreat at high speed.

* * * * * ○ * * * *

CHAPTER 30

The Blizzard or How I Survived Eleven Days and Nights Snowed in With Three Children, a Cat, a Dog, Possible Appendicitis, a Head Cold and — Sometimes — a Husband

Before marriage, my perception of winter was that it was a sometimes beautiful, sometimes ugly time of year. Blizzards came and went, and there were snow plows and transit systems, stores within easy reach and no one depending on me. Living in the country, being married and having a family changed my perception.

Country winter is hoping that when the children get on the bus at 7:30 A.M., under dark but clear skies, that they won't be held captive at the school by a surprise blizzard.

Country winter is waking up in the morning when it's still dark and finding that one reason for the dark is not only the early hour, but also the fact that all the windows and doors are piled to the top with snowdrifts.

Country winter is keeping the snow shovel standing against the wall in the living room, because the wind sweeping across the lake piles snow into high drifts that have a tendency to lean against the storm door and we know we'll have to shovel from the inside out by removing the glass.

Country winter is climbing up on the roof (without having to use a ladder — just climb the drifts) and shovelling and shovelling because, though blood may be thicker than water, that light, feathery, white stuff out there is heavier than the roof, and you'd better believe it.

Winter was almost over. It was March — the second Tuesday in March. Time to think ahead to crocus, spring cleaning and getting out the lawnmower.

But March is deceptive. A storm was brewing, according to the weather report, and when Billy, Joey and Linda bounded off the school bus, they ran into the house, full of the good news and hoping for no school the next day.

I shrugged. Just another storm. So what? Of course there would be school. I was so unconcerned I didn't even go for groceries. "I'll wait for the sales circular to come in the morning," I said to Renaud. "I want to see what the specials are." I didn't know it, but it wasn't the time to be thrifty.

That night, as I set the alarm clock, I looked with some concern at Renaud shivering under the quilts. He obviously had a fever.

"Maybe we won't get snow at all," I said comfortingly, turning away to look out at the clear, star-filled night. But I was wrong. By midnight we had been plunged with a vengeance into a howling winter-fury of a storm.

All night the winds dumped snow over our house in drifts with the momentum that only four miles of flat, frozen lake can allow. By morning the car was buried, the house was running a close second and the highway had disappeared, outlined only by a row of hydro poles sticking out above the drifts. We were snowbound.

I called Arnold, the school-bus driver. "Don't come for my kids today," I told him.

"I didn't intend to," said Arnold. "I can't even see my bus."

While I prepared breakfast in a leisurely way — nobody was going to be rushing out of the house — the children leaped out of bed enthusiastically (remember, no school) to check the progress of the storm. "OOOooohh, lookit all that snow!" they whooped, racing from snow-packed window to snow-packed window.

From the upstairs bedroom window Renaud peered glumly at the billows of powdered snow sweeping over the tops of giant, wave-like drifts. He had work to do at the office, and the prospect of being snowed in was not an inviting one.

After an unhurried breakfast, punctuated by occasional expressions of joy from the small fry and trapped sounds from the man of the house, a roar rising above the storm launched Renaud to his feet with an expression that could only be interpreted as one of profound hope. Rescue?

It was Arthur, our grader operator. We watched as he left the grader and waded through the drift in our driveway. He cleared his way to the door and came in, announcing that he'd worked all night clearing roads; there was nothing else on the road anywhere. "Do you have any cognac?" he asked.

As he sipped, smoked and crouched near the fireplace, Arthur added that the only part of the road cleared was what he had just done with the grader, and even that was closing in as fast as it was opened.

Renaud was disappointed, but quickly rallied, deciding to ride in the grader with Arthur the six miles to the garage.

"But Renaud," I pleaded, "you can't go out in that storm with your cold."

"Don't worry," he said.

"But you're sick."

"Aw — what's a little cold?"

A little cold? After all, he hadn't exactly been suffering in silence up to now with his little cold.

"Besides," he continued. "I'll be inside the grader cab with Arthur. We'll be O.K."

"But if you get stuck on the road . . ."

"Don't worry, I'm fine."

"But . . ."

"Margie dear . . ."

They finished their cognac and Renaud scrambled into a snowmobile suit and boots, mentally outlining his day's work.

That's all very well for them, I thought bitterly, as Renaud wrapped a scarf around his neck an put on thick mittens. Well, not that I wanted to go along with them in the grader, but I did resent Renaud escaping our housebound household.

Renaud and Arthur didn't have such an easy escape. They were only able to ride out the blizzard for about four miles before bogging down in the two-storey-high drifts at Dupuis's Corner, two miles short of the garage.

Three hours later, Renaud phoned from the garage to let me know he had arrived all right. "The road," he croaked between coughs (but cheerfully, because he was at work), "is totally blocked." He added that they'd had to abandon the grader and he and Arthur had stumbled, crawled and even rolled the two miles from there to the garage. He would spend the night next door with his parents. I was not to worry.

The next morning the drifts crossing the road in front of our house were even higher, which brought forth more cheers from the willingly captive boys. Linda, who was now sick, smiled wanly and drifted off into fevered sleep.

After breakfast and a rousing game of Monopoly with the boys, I took inventory. Because of my earlier compulsion to be thrifty and wait for the sales circular from the store, the shelves were not bristling with cans and packages. At least the freezer was solvent, with one turkey, thirty-five pounds of chicken, two pounds of bacon and several quarts of frozen fruit.

We also had half a loaf of bread, twenty pounds of milk powder, twenty pounds of flour, ten pounds of sugar, some oatmeal, a lot of potatoes, two cans of Bravo sauce, four cans of corn, one can of Chinese noodles, some rice, a twenty-five pound bag of dog food and a half dozen cans of cat food.

The novelty of schoolless freedom finally began to wane for the boys, and between refereeing their fights, preparing meals, taking Linda's temperature and looking dejectedly out at the storm, I called some friends to find out if they were snowed in (they were); if their husbands hated being snowed in (they did); if they were getting fed up with their husbands (they were); and if the children were giving them the screaming meamies (you can say that again). I felt infinitely better.

For lunch we had chicken.

For supper we had chicken.

By now the protective sheet of plastic over the picture window facing the lake was flapping in shreds, and a mini-snowdrift was forming across the braided rug. Occasional looks out the upstairs window were not encouraging. I felt detached. It was as though we were in a little oasis beyond which there was nothing but snow.

I unwisely wondered aloud about the possibility of power failure. Billy and Joey thought that would add something to our situation and dug out their camp equipment, our old oil lamp, which contained no oil, our portable gas camp stove, which contained no gas, and candles — four two-inch stubs.

In the spirit of giving them something to think about I asked, "What would we do about heat?" I knew that the woodpile by the fireplace would not last long and the outside woodpile was buried under at least fifteen feet of snow. They weren't discouraged, and spent a giddy half-hour discussing which pieces of furniture should be the first to go. If worse came to worse, they declared solemnly, they would even sacrifice their school books to keep us warm. At least the oil heater was operating on an almost full tank.

I looked in on Linda, who was now having severe pains in the lower abdomen. After she threw up her light supper of chicken soup and crackers I turned to the medical book. Appendix? It couldn't be. I considered a heroic fourteen-mile journey by snowmobile over open country, in this blizzard, to the hospital. It was a good time to develop a headache.

I swallowed two aspirin, dropped a brick on rising hysteria and called Doctor Cameron, who listened carefully, asked questions, then reassured me, "There's a lot of that going around." It wasn't her appendix, but a new flu bug thriving in the area.

The boys watched the late movie on TV, fighting during commercial breaks. They ate the last of the popcorn before staggering to the bathroom to brush their teeth and tumbling into bed.

I didn't have the heart to evict Linda, Putt-Putt and Happy from the master bedroom, so I threw sheets, quilts and pillow on the living-room sofa and retired. Sort of. The storm continued. I dozed occasionally, leaping up at intervals during the night to check on Linda and look out at the snow swirling high around the tops of the windows.

Morning finally came with no untoward events, in spite of my foreboding: What if the big window facing the lake breaks? What if the house catches fire? Again no snow plows. Sounds of the blizzard were muted by the insulation of thick snow. The downstairs windows, except for about six inches near the top of the living-room window, were completely buried and made the house dark as night. It was suffocatingly like living in a cave.

So far the storm had brought twenty-four inches of snow, which high winds had piled into twenty-two-foot drifts.

The front door was the only one we could use — and that only by removing the storm window. I lifted out the glass, reached out and cleared enough snow away from the door with the shovel to be able to open it. Several times a day I cleared the door to let Happy out. Every time he came back in he shook snow from his long fur and rubbed himself dry on the braided rug. Putt-Putt didn't have a problem — for the duration of the storm she used a cat-pan.

I did some neglected house cleaning, like cupboards, closets and drawers. Then the children woke up and after breakfast I got bogged down in juvenile hostilities. Then the water pipes to the kitchen froze. I was fed up with the housework anyway, so I settled down with a hot lemonade and a stack of books.

It was a good idea, but as soon as I got comfortable, Joey stepped on the rim of the dog's water dish, flinging the contents across the kitchen. Then Billy stuck his finger into a narrow-necked earthenware cruet and couldn't get it out. I gave up, abandoning the lemonade and books to become a participant, which didn't reduce the number of crises, but at least I could see them coming and was already on my feet.

For lunch we had chicken.

For supper we had chicken.

On the fourth day, Renaud called, still coughing, to say that he couldn't get home and would stay with his parents again.

The children and I watched some TV late news that scrolled a printed list of 369 places in the city that would be closed next day. "Hurrah!" the boys chorused.

"Thanks a lot . . ." I said grimly.

The boys were happy, Happy, HAPPY! Morning brought no change.

It was Saturday. Butter almost gone, also eggs, coffee and detergent. On a more concentrated search of the kitchen cupboards I found yeast and made a batch of bread, using bacon drippings instead of oil.

For lunch we had chicken.

For supper we had chicken.

The storm was calming; Linda's temperature went down. After supper Renaud called, said the municipal plow had just passed by and he would get a ride with his brother Maurice and follow it home.

"Call the grocery store and give them an order," said Renaud. "I'll stop in to pick it up on the way home."

This was better. Being snowed in with three active children is one thing, but having them hungry at the same time was not something I cared to think about.

When I called the store I was told that the villagers within walking distance had emptied the shelves, and new supplies couldn't get in until the roads opened.

"We can manage, I'm sure," I said to Renaud when he got home.

"Maybe, but from what I understand," he said, blowing his nose, "there's another storm on the way tonight."

I laughed heartily. What a sense of humor that husband of mine has. Another storm indeed.

It was so good to have Renaud home again. I missed him. After the children were in bed that evening, Renaud and I settled cosily on the sofa to listen to the late news on TV. "At least another six inches of snow tonight," the commentator said cheerfully, "with winds gusting to fifty miles per hour. Stay off the road, folks!" Yeah, well . . .

"It'll miss us," I told Renaud.

"Sure it will," he said, coughing deeply a few times. "Sure it will."

The next morning I could hardly wait to run to the upstairs

window and be reassured. Instead, there it was, another full-fledged blizzard.

This may not sound reasonable, but remember when I expressed resentment that Renaud had got away earlier in the storm, leaving me stranded with the children? Well, I didn't know what I was talking about because if there's one thing worse than being snowed-in with the children and animals, it's having a husband included in the bargain — no matter how much you really love each other.

Not that Renaud isn't reasonable, it's just that he doesn't take graciously to enforced captivity. Neither do I, but at least I don't have to watch myself pacing back and forth, looking at dust on the furniture, examining cobwebs in corners and picking dog hairs off the sofa.

Also, from his wing-back chair in the living room, Renaud can observe the whole household at a glance. Though why he should want to is beyond me.

As the day progressed (or deteriorated) I worked about in the kitchen like a nervous bride. With Renaud's critical eye on me I peeled potatoes, dropping them on the floor. I filled the dog's water dish and spilled it and lost my grip on the thawing turkey, which shot across the table and, of course, thudded to the floor. I dropped a cup, nicked myself with the vegetable knife, tripped over the rug in front of the sink, spilled the sugar and yelled at the dog, who finished his dinner of leftovers and then parked in the middle of the kitchen floor, where he amused himself by lunging at his metal food dish, playing tiddly-winks with it as violently as possible. Happy was in usually good spirits and his endurance was far superior to mine as he swatted, walloped and catapulted his dish through the air to ricochet off the fridge, cupboard and, finally, my shins.

By now Linda had re-joined the indoor community, wrapped in a patchwork quilt. The three kids passed the time fighting over who had more orange juice, who'd cheated at Monopoly, who'd sneaked the last of the Sugar Crisp, and who'd spilled the cough syrup.

They fought over who had the good chair in front of the TV first and who stole Billy's chocolate bar, which he had hidden under his pillow — a question that was easily answered when Joey suggested we smell Happy's breath.

A lively game of Ping-Pong at the kitchen table didn't help much; neither did a game of hockey in the living room when Renaud got an off-the-coffee-table rebound in the gut and asked me stringently if I couldn't *do something* about the children (he used to say he wanted eleven) and did I have to *let* them play hockey in the house?

I swept up a shattered fruit bowl, warned the children that I was getting to the end of my rope and sneaked off to the bathroom for a brief five-minute cry — which really wasn't enough, but had to do.

Renaud finally escaped to work when his friend Pierre stopped by on his snowmobile. As a parting shot I warned him to be wary of opening the door if and when he managed to get back home, because more than likely my nerves would have to be peeled off the ceiling by then. He looked at me blankly, trying to decide if the matter was worth pursuing, decided it wasn't, gave me a farewell peck on the cheek and took off like a bat out of hell.

By the time Renaud came home that night, the village store had received a truckload of supplies via the cleared highway west of the village, but the store was closed. I admired Renaud's ingenuity at getting away and his devotion for coming back home, but I couldn't say much for his timing.

For lunch we had turkey. The one that had fallen on the floor.

For supper we had turkey with rice.

Monday the weather improved, but the roads were still blocked.

When Arthur got through with the grader again, Renaud took Billy with him to the garage, then called to tell me that farmers had had to throw out thousands of gallons of milk because the bulk tank trucks couldn't get through. Now they were working on the sideroads and highways with tractor-mounted blowers in an effort to clear them for the tank trucks. Three barns in the area had caved in from the weight of accumulated snow, and a few summer cottages along the lakeshore had followed suit.

By Tuesday my routine cold merged with an oppressive case of cabin-fever, for which there was no cure in sight.

Wednesday the schools were still closed, but at least the power hadn't gone off.

The schools opened Thursday, but the buses couldn't get through to our house yet. By Saturday the sun was shining hotly. I walked up the narrow path the boys had cleared to the top of the driveway, and looking back from there, I could just see the tip of our roof.

Sunday we picked up our cameras and stepped out into the blinding white sunshine to record for posterity the unbelievable drifts and narrow snowmobile trail weaving past our almost buried home. Renaud said, "We should be back to normal by tomorrow." Joey added, "Wow! When this melts . . ."

It lasted eleven days. The children may never want to eat chicken again, and I made a reminder note to get gas for the camp stove, oil for the lamp, wood for the fireplace and lots of candles. But there's no rush. After all, we're not likely to get another storm like that, are we? Well . . . are we?

CHAPTER 31

* * * * ○ * * * *

In Sickness and in Health

It's fish hooks,
   and tonsils,
      it's scrapes and falls and bruises.

It's chicken-pox,
   and whooping-cough,
      and sunburns, boils, contusions.

It's comforting and
   cleaning up,
      and bandaging of sprains.

It's waiting for
   the doc to call
      and walking with a cane.

When Renaud and I got married, I had little experience with medical matters.

As a matter of fact, if I thought about illness at all, it would have been in the romantic sense of comforting and reassuring — you know, the cool-hand-to-the-fevered-brow sort of thing — conjuring up images of Elizabeth Barrett Browning and Florence Nightingale.

189

Then we had children, and I discovered that the advent of childhood diseases in the Caza compound involved an added dimension, since I was in the family. I had missed most of those plagues during my sheltered childhood and had always considered myself very lucky and probably immune.

I was not right in either instance, because when the children entered school, I entered my second childhood. They got the measles, I got the measles. They got whooping-cough, I got whooping-cough. They got chicken-pox, I got chicken-pox.

I not only got their ailments, usually at the same time they did, but also had to stay on my feet to clean up after their frequent violent upheavals.

Good ol' Renaud remained unaffected. Having grown up with many brothers and sisters, he'd been through all this years before and simply shook his head in resignation whenever he came home from work to find the epidemic blanket lowered over the Caza household.

I, on the other hand, wandered around the house for days, clutching a thermometer, scrub-bucket, sponge and bottles of cough syrup and Dr. Fowler's Extract of Wild Strawberry.

Ministering to the ills of the children and myself was one thing, but getting Renaud to seek medical attention was as easy as persuading him to hand-feed piranha fish. When he slammed the hood of the truck on his thumb, when he cut his hand at the garage, when a battery blew up in his face, when he injured his leg in a fall, he always insisted that he was fine and didn't need help.

Even when he helped my parents get acquainted with their new power lawnmower and mowed off the tips of three fingers, all he wanted to do was gather up the children, put a plastic bread bag over his dripping bandage and drive home.

Home was thirty miles away, and that's where he wanted

to be. No, he did not want me to drive the car. No, he would not go to a doctor. Yes, he intended to drive all the way home, through city traffic, bleeding all the way. No, he would not call a doctor first. He was fine. Just fine.

By the time we got out of the city I was so upset that he agreed to stop at a doctor's house. But the babysitter said the doctor was at a dinner party and not expected home until late. Satisfied that he had now done his duty, Renaud drove the rest of the way home and declared that he was going to bed and to sleep. He was tired, he said.

It's a fact of life that when a wife asks a husband to do something that makes sense, he says, "No." But if a comparative stranger suggests the same thing he suddenly becomes docile and follows orders. As soon as Renaud was safely in bed, I sneaked to the nearest of our neighbors who still had their lights on, and they routed Renaud out of bed and drove him to a doctor a few miles away. Renaud spent the next few days in hospital for skin graft operations.

I also discovered that perfectly normal medical procedures are not always normal to an anxious mother awaiting a young son's return from the operating room without his tonsils. By the time Joey was wheeled back to his room, deep concern combined with the stale, zinging smell of the operating room and Mother went out like a light.

I discovered that most medical situations are of the "surprise, surprise" variety, like the time Renaud got pinned to the cab of the float by the blade of his bulldozer while it was being loaded in a January blizzard. It had him pinned across the upper chest. There was a crunch as bone broke. Someone yelled to the operator, the bulldozer scrambled into reverse and Renaud was taken to hospital.

It was a relief when he was safely home again, but let me tell you, winter is no time to be confined to the house with an injured husband. Renaud was hurt in body, but not sick in the sense that he was languishing in bed with a raging fever to drowse the hours away. He was more like a bear with a sore paw.

He spent the next couple of weeks miserably housebound, uncomfortable and unable to drive, with an ongoing winter storm outside and nothing more entertaining to do than watch Miss Veronica's "Romper Room" on our ancient TV set that could tune into only two channels.

While we don't have more medical problems than anyone else, I'm still curious as to why a man will give up the single life of freedom for the debts, responsibilities, well-being and never-ending needs of a family. There he is, earning a good salary, coming and going as he chooses, with only himself to buy food and clothing for.

Then one day he and an almost complete stranger say, "I do." And he buys a house and becomes a debt-ridden family man.

And don't forget those times when everything hits the fan at once. I'll never forget the week I went to Toronto where my father was scheduled for open-heart surgery. The day before I left, Joey complained of leg pain. Both legs. I called Dr. Cameron, drove Joey to the hospital for X-rays, and was told he needed a plaster cast first on one leg from ankle to thigh for six weeks, then ditto for the other leg.

When I came back from Toronto I broke a tooth, then got a boil on my chin. Billy came down with the flu, Linda developed sinusitis, Joey got an ear infection, my annual check-up came due, then Joey fell down stairs at school, cracked his cast and had to go back to hospital for repairs.

I was maneuvering by cane myself at this point, awaiting foot surgery, and as I hobbled along I ducked my head when I shouldn't have and got a black eye from the corner of the cupboard door. Then I ran the sewing machine needle through my finger while fixing the zipper on a pair of jeans in a hurry (it hurt, but not as much as I'd always been afraid it might), and while doing the laundry, I reached into the washer too soon and caught my thumbnail in the spinner.

It was a dreadful month of one thing after another, and it wasn't finished yet because while rushing to answer the telephone in the dark, I stepped on a dog bone in my bare feet, and the next morning my good watch slipped off the shelf over the sink and lazed around in the bottom of the soapy water in the dishpan until I found it when the dishes were finished. That one couldn't be called sickness, but it surely made me sick.

As if that weren't enough I had a suspicion that Putt-Putt was pregnant, and I could feel the tingle of a cold sore coming on.

We were worried about religious differences? The name of this game was Survival.

How can a man let himself in for such a commitment as family life? Come to think of it, what am *I* doing here?!

CHAPTER 32

* * * * * ○ * * * *

Hot Coffee through a Straw

It was my turn to go to hospital. An injured bone in my foot. For four years nobody could agree, and I was told, "Really, it couldn't be that painful." (It was.) "That must be very painful." (See.) "It's an arthritic growth." (It wasn't.) "It's definitely not an arthritic growth." (See.) "Lots of people have those things." (You want to bet?) "Here, how about some cortisone shots right into the heel — let's say a series of five, and we'll see what that does."

The only thing it did was make me unpleasant to live with.

Finally I was sent to a specialist, then admitted to a Montreal hospital where I became aware that my troubles were few and small compared to those of the people around me.

I opted for a four-bed room and met Mary, who had had hip surgery two days earlier; Irene, who was due for spinal fusion; and Connie, who was waiting for hip surgery.

My operation was scheduled for the next morning, so my foot was prepared, then wrapped in yards of sterile cotton.

At 10:00 P.M. a nurse came around and told me that the cigarette I was smoking was my last (which sounded ominous). I was instructed in deep breathing and coughing. I was told that the operation would be at 9:00 A.M., that I was to drink nothing after midnight and that I was to have a good sleep.

In the morning I was delivered to X-ray, then taken back to my room for final scrub before being shipped to the operating room. It was so easy — not at all like having a baby, where you are expected to do a lot of the work yourself. One minute I was lying there chatting with my doctor; the next minute someone was telling me to wake up and I was in recovery. It was over.

But the total experience wasn't over — not yet.

Before surgery, the therapist had come in and measured me for crutches. Within hours of the surgery I was expected to try them, bringing to light a piece of advice nobody told me — be prepared for a lot of aches and pains where you don't expect them. Lying down on unyielding surfaces for surgery and using previously unused muscles (neck-raisers, hip-shifters) afterwards can make every bone and muscle hurt. Which doesn't make any hospital duty easier — especially therapy.

> A lot can be said,
> for a hospital bed:
> It's hard and
> too high from the ground.
> When you try to get there
> with crutch levered in air,
> you're likely to land
>   uʍop ǝpᴉsdn

"Here — just hold the crutches by this cross-bar," the therapist said cheerily, "and lower yourself to the floor."

"O.K.," I said, and did as she asked.

"Not like that!" she yelped, as I slid off the bed and the crutch uppers caught me under the arms, raising my shoulders to ear level and almost sweeping both feet entirely clear of the floor.

"What do I do now?" I asked, dangling limply while stars and black specks flashed furiously in front of my eyes, sweat poured down my forehead, the back of my neck became hot and damp and my ears buzzed.

The therapist looked rather shaken. "Well, don't do that again," she said. "Let's see if you can take just a couple of steps, then you'd better get back into bed. I can't understand it," she continued nervously. "I measured you for those crutches myself, but they're much too long for you."

"I know," I said weakly. "You see, I'm much taller stretched out flat."

"What?" she asked.

"When I stand up," I said, "I tend to accordion somewhat. You measured me while I was lying flat."

Unable to catch the humor in this, the therapist said "Huummmm," and led me back to the bed. "Now," she instructed briskly, "just hop right up on this footstool, turn around and sit on the bed."

"You've got to be kidding," I protested. My heart was still pounding and my ears were still buzzing. Surely she didn't expect me to lever myself into mid-air on those two spindly sticks of wood. That was exactly what she did expect, though. And I did it, but it sure felt like a full day's work. I crawled into bed, lay back and watched the ceiling until suppertime.

When supper came, Irene lifted the lid of her dish, immediately slapped it down again and declared that she was afraid her supper was alive. A second look exposed what turned out to be a dish called "creamed egg on rusk," of which she ate half, then telephoned her husband and told him to stop at the Colonel's and bring some chicken with him on his evening visit.

Connie, Mary and I had chosen the sliced cold roast beef, which Connie said should be sent for diagnosis and Mary thought was ready for autopsy. I thought it deserved an immediate burial.

What's all this fuss about a private room? Four to a room is much more fun!

On the seventh day of my stay, I was sent for a myelogram, a test of the spine where they inject dye into the spinal column and follow its travels to outline damaged areas.

The young doctor in charge shook my confidence by constantly asking questions of the technician at the X-ray console. "Where's the foot control? Doesn't this one have a foot control?" "How do you make this thing turn?" "Where is the lever for this end?" and "Is a Number 18 needle all right to use, because the only thing here is an 18, and I thought I was supposed to use a Number 20."

After half an hour of this and being bumped on the head three times by the overhanging apparatus as I was raised and lowered, plus four jabs to find the right place for the needle, the technician came out of the booth and addressed the young doctor. "Say, are you new here?" The doctor smiled proudly and told her that he had just started yesterday, whereupon I came close to falling off the down-tilted table.

After the test, I was wheeled back to my bed and told that if I didn't want a miserable spinal headache, I was not to move from a flat position for twenty-four hours.

It's not easy to adjust to horizontal living when you've always been vertical. First there was the matter of peas on the supper tray. I started out with a fork, but the peas rolled down into my ears and behind my neck. There was the matter of soup, too, which I gave up on right away. Eating tomato rice soup through a straw seemed to be just asking for death as the clogged mass hits the back of the windpipe. At least I was in the right place for such an event.

Coffee was another matter. Drinking hot coffee through a straw simply delivered the hot, without the taste. The whole business was very tiring.

Eager as I was to get home, I had reservations about my strength. I was going home, on crutches, to a husband, three kids, a cat and dog and a house. It was scary.

Renaud came to get me, and we arrived back home just in time for the school bus fallout. A quick cup of coffee, then Renaud told the children, "Take good care of Mommie," and hurried back to work.

While I was definitely away from home, it was remarkable how self-sufficient my little brood could be, but Mother at home is Mother at home, whether traveling on one foot or two, so Joey collapsed in front of the television, Billy collected his fishing gear and raced off to the pier and Linda yelled, "Whoopie!" and flew out of the door with Happy. I stood there looking at the dirtiest floor in Canada and a sour-smelling dish towel that gave the appearance of having been used as a floor mop.

"It's the last one," Linda explained cheerfully when I questioned her about it. "All the others are in the bathtub." (With two weeks' worth of other laundry). I almost asked how they took their baths while I was away, but thought better of it. I didn't want to know.

The house was airless. The storm windows were still on, and two weeks' worth of garbage bags (full and ripe) sat in a corner of the kitchen smelling bad.

All the brave resolutions made while I was in hospital, about not being a burden on my family, crumbled. The feeling seemed to be that Mom is home, so things are back to normal.

Not that I wasn't willing, but my first mistake was trying to carry a carton of milk from the refrigerator to the table by holding it under my chin. Then I tried to mop the milk off the floor and got the mop tangled in the crutches. Impossible.

Finally I stood in the middle of the kitchen and called for all hands on deck in an effort to get things ship-shape before Renaud came home for supper.

The children, disappointed, realized that good ol' Mom was not up to anything more strenuous than lifting a small cup of coffee, and they were still on their own.

* * * * ○ * * * *

CHAPTER 33

Walk Alone Together

Did Renaud and I think about the future when we decided to get married? Perhaps, in a rosy, idealized way. Like young people in love who talk about celebrating future landmark anniversaries.

I'm sure I daydreamed about an adoring husband, a sweet little cottage and darling, tractable babies who would throw their arms around my neck and say, "Mommie, I love you."

Just so did I perceive Renaud and I growing closer as the years went smoothly by. We did grow closer, though not because the years went by smoothly, because they didn't. There were some mighty rough spots along the way. Why wouldn't there be? It's part of the texture that makes the tapestry of life interesting . . . enduring.

As for being a parent, that was not easy for either of us. When we married, Renaud — although a veteran of large-family living, growing up surrounded by din and companionship — may have been more used to noise and surging humanity, but he had no more callouses of experience than I when it came to the challenges of *raising* a family.

Our lives changed, almost overnight, from a dreamy self-centeredness to being caught in the rush to provide the physical necessities and tend to the growing needs and wants of the children, each other, the business, the house, the pets and the community. We spent the next couple of decades doing things right, doing things wrong, worrying, telling the children we loved them and gritting out through clenched teeth, "No, that's final, you can't join the Peace Corps at twelve."

Being a parent was an astonishing, confusing and rewarding jumble of experiences. It was a circus. A stage play. A clutter of split-second decisions, mistakes and consequences.

We, the idealistic, anxious and inexperienced, who had so many doubts and fears ourselves, were now supposed to assuage doubts and fears in our children, instill moral values, imbue with confidence and then stand aside as our handiwork walked away from our protective custody.

Then suddenly there were no more children in the house. Well, they were our children still, of course, but gone were the baby curls, chubby hands, tumble of shrill, happy voices and childlike dependence. Instead there were graduations, cars, motorboats, romantic attachments and the right to vote.

That sounds like a terribly big jump, but in reality, it happened gradually, except for those landmark leaps of insight. Like when our first-born came back from college one afternoon, covertly wrestling with one of life's grown-up problems newly burdening his young shoulders. I watched, and just as I was about to reach out sympathetically to pat the dejected shoulder — to squeeze the defeated hand, to speak a word of comfort — I saw a tear that might embarrass if discovered. A little-boy vulnerability in the manly young face. My arms ached to hold him close and my heart ached even more, but I knew that, difficult as it surely was, I must pretend I didn't notice. Must leave him to recover from his personal wounds and save his important pride.

The first time we felt the impact of all our children reaching for the freedom that comes with young adulthood was on a beautiful August Sunday. Sailboats and canoes skimmed over the lake. Snatches of music drifted from the cottages and barbecue aromas mingled richly with the scent of sun-warmed countryside.

Renaud and I sat out on lawn chairs, listening to the occasional burst of laughter and bright chatter rolling pleasantly along the shoreline of the bay as our neighbors relaxed in their weekend escape from the city's heat.

Sunday suppers in our house are lively and informal occasions. Open house — more or less. The children know they can bring someone home for supper and the welcome will be warm and the food plentiful. I had roasted a turkey and made a lemon meringue pie. But on this particular summer Sunday, not only did the children fail to turn up with visitors for supper, but Bill, now twenty, and with his own car, went off to the mountains with five carloads of friends. Joey, eighteen, left in our car to meet his friend Victor, trading roast turkey for pizza and disco, and Linda, fifteen, threw a change of clothes into her knapsack and left with our new summer neighbors to stay the night in the city with them and their daughter Anne-Marie.

It had never happened before. Here we were, with an extension leaf in the dining room table, a twenty-four-pound turkey with all the trimmings, and just the two of us.

It was a moment of truth. Proof that the family does grow up and away — though the whole process was so gradual that the time between their births and independence telescoped into a sort of noisy, sweet, colorful blur. By the time the dust settled, there we were, Renaud and I, facing each other over that big bird.

It's a bit like learning to drive a car, driving it for twenty years, then losing your licence. The car is still around, mind you, and you love that car, but you can no longer drive it — and chances are it's sitting in someone else's driveway anyway.

So it's time to let go of one part of life and get on with another. I don't mean time to saunter dejectedly into the golden years, but time to perceive that the spirit feeds not only on determination and hard work, but on a good sense of fun as well — and to realize that, though each person walks alone through the strange lot of experiences that comprise life in general and marriage in particular, walking alone is far better done in good company.